PULLING THROUGH

by

Eileen Marie

Table of Contents

First and foremost,

I dedicate this book to my husband,

who has been so patient and understanding

throughout our marriage.

This book also is dedicated to the following:

Kurt Opprecht, for his patience, understanding and leadership.

Lara, for her review, opinions and advice.

A special thank you to Teri for her unwavering faith in making me believe that this book could be accomplished, encouraging me to follow through and for the many hours she spent reviewing my work.

Also to all the women who have walked in my path and fear no shadows.

THIS IS MY LIFE STORY

ALL EVENTS CITED IN THIS STORY
ARE BASED ON TRUE FACTS

All of the names within this story have
been changed in order to maintain the
privacy of others.

PROLOGUE

I am now eleven years old. Approximately three months after my sisters moved to town, an unthinkable horrible episode occurs. I am sleeping soundly and suddenly waken in the middle of the night with my father lying in bed beside me attempting to fondle my breast. I can smell the alcohol from his breath. I try to move away but to no avail since I am being pushed against the wall. He proceeds to grope between my legs into my private area. I do not know what is happening; I try to move away from him and this is when he tears off my pajama bottom, gets on top of me. I don't understand what is happening, except that he is really hurting me.

My father is very intelligent, as well as devious, cunning and sly. He is well aware that I lack knowledge of his actions, that I am so fearful of abuses and have a total lack of self-confidence due to the foster home's physical and psychological abuses; therefore he knows just how he can play on my fears using them against me with a devised plan.

He says, "I have something important to tell you, and I don't want you to be upset. When I made love to you, which is what I did the other night, I found out that something horrible must have happened to you while you were living in the first foster home". He then says, "Do you remember your foster Papa touching you and forcing himself on you?"

CHAPTER 1

THE ORPHANAGE

My very first memory is living in a large home with several children, including my brothers and sisters; I was a little over three years old at the time. I do not realize that I am an orphan, nor do I understand why I now live in what everyone calls an orphanage with my sisters and brothers. What is an orphanage? My mother and father are nowhere to be found, and I cannot understand where they have gone and why they left us. I keep asking "where is Mommy?" All my siblings can do is look at me and either cry, try to change the subject, or keep me occupied. Then, finally as I get a few months older, I have given up hope that Mommy will return. I approach my brother Norman, who is my favorite because of his patience and willingness to take time to help me.

I ask him, "Where is Mommy, and why can't I find her?"

"Mom is in Heaven," he replies.

I ask, "Where is Heaven?"

He explains the following: "Heaven is where God lives, Mom died and since she was such a good person, she went to join God in heaven, she cannot come back, but remember she will always look down on us and will be so proud when we behave. She will always be with us in our mind, so we will never forget her. I know we cannot see her; we can talk to her and she will listen, she cannot talk back, but just to have her listen is very important to us." Although I do not fully understand, I now know Mommy will never return and I am so sad, and feel so lost. I decide to do what Norman suggests; I am now starting to secretly talk to her every night and although I miss her so much, I know she is listening to me and that makes me feel a little better, now I can tell her all my secrets.

I am the youngest child of a family of fourteen, born on my mother's thirtieth birthday in September of 1935. Although my mother gave birth to fourteen children, five of my siblings had already passed away when I was born. There are no details available about the death of the other five children, but since we were poor and medical attention was not readily available, it is probable that illnesses took those young lives.

It was December of 1938 when Mother passed away leaving a family of nine children. My father is not around, nor do I remember him being available or visiting us, however I do not notice his absence; since my mother is the one I really miss. My oldest sister, Ellen, is sixteen, which is past the age of admittance for the orphanage and has been left to fend for herself.   I ask my brother Norman,

"Where is Daddy and how come he is not here with us?"

Norman replies, "Dad has to go to work and his work is not around here, but he may come back for us later on", that seems to satisfy me, but I still wonder how come he never comes to see us. I am later told that he disappeared and it was learned that the orphanage was reimbursed by our grandfather, for our upkeep.

Two of my siblings, my sister Leanne, who is eleven months older than me, and my brother Robert, who is two years older and I are inseparable, we are the three youngest and are seldom apart.

I wake up from my afternoon nap one day, look for Leanne and Robert and cannot find them. At first I think they are playing a game on me and are hiding; I think they must have finally found a very good hiding place, but then I soon become concerned since both Robert and Leanne are nowhere around; I start thinking that they may have decided to join Mommy in heaven. I ask Norman, "Have you seen Leanne or Robert?"

He looks at me with a very sad face and says, "Yes, they were taken away by foster parents, and I have no idea where their new home will be located."

I say, "What are foster parents?"

He replies, "They are mothers and fathers who want to adopt orphans like us, that means, take them into their home and be their mothers and fathers."

I am devastated, I do not believe him and keep looking for both of them for several days then finally I realize and accept what Norman has told me; they are gone. I am so sad, because again, not only have I lost my mother, now I have lost my best sister and brother and I did not even have a chance to say goodbye. Within just a few months, I have lost family members that I loved the most. Although my other siblings have tried to explain that Leanne and Robert found a better home, I still cannot understand why they would have agreed to go to another home with other parents, when they had a good home with all of us.

CHAPTER 2

FOSTER HOME

A few months after Robert and Leanne disappeared, a couple who had heard what had happened to our family drove three hundred miles to the orphanage, hoping to adopt one of us girls. Three hundred miles is a long way to drive in the 1930's. Why had they come so far? There were certainly children in need closer to their home. Whatever their reasons and their needs, they arrive at the orphanage to meet each of us girls individually. When it was my turn, they told me to sit down and they ask me, "Do you know why you are here?"

I say, "I am here because my mother went away to heaven, and I am now waiting for her to send for me, because I miss her so much, I want to join her". That is the extent of the conversation.

They then go to the other room to talk to the orphanage sisters; and when they return they say, "Come Aileen, you are the one we have chosen to travel with us."

In a matter of hours, I am shuffled off to live with this couple. I am not allowed to say goodbye to my brothers, Will, Norm, Vick and my sisters, Rose, and Joan. No one bothers to explain to me what is happening and I am so scared. Before I realize what is going on, I find myself in these stranger's car, being driven away from everyone dear to me. The drive is taking such a long time that I fall asleep. When I awaken, I am still in the car with strangers; I am so scared and unhappy; I start crying and do not understand why this is happening. The lady sitting in the front seat of the car seems to get very frustrated with me and she finally says, "Stop that crying, you should be happy to be with us; we are now your parents and you are to call us Papa and Maman; you are being taken to your new home and you will be living with us from now on. We have two sons, Ron and John, which you will meet when we arrive home and you will be part of our family, so behave yourself and stop crying." Her voice seems so harsh as I sit in the back seat and I do not fully understand what is going on, except that I am being taken further away from my brothers and sisters and will now be living with strangers.

Then I overhear my new foster Maman say to my new foster Papa, "We should go and visit Phillip and Angeline soon, so that Aileen can be reunited with Leanne and Robert." As soon as I hear those words, I realize they know the people who took my brother and sister. I perk up and cannot wait to reach our destination. Although I do not know who Phillip and Angeline are, I want to see my brother and sister as soon as possible.

When we arrive at their home, they take me into the house, and I do not see Leanne nor Robert, so I say to my new Maman, "Where is Leanne?" I receive no response. Again, I feel so alone and although I do not fully understand the reason for having been taken away from the orphanage, I now fully realize that I will be living in a new home and will no longer see my family.

My new parents live in the Province of Quebec. Since my language is totally French, I am fortunate that the only language spoken in Quebec is French. My last name is being changed from Charet to the foster family's name of Gaspar; however no legal papers are filed for this transition. The foster parents already have two sons, Ron who is eight years, has brown hair and blue eyes, and has a quick smile and a pleasant personality. John is six, has reddish hair with blue eyes, and appears more serious than Ron.

When I first meet their two sons, it seems so strange, especially since Ron says, "Hello little girl, welcome, we will be your brothers from now on and you will be sharing a bedroom with John and I."

I tell them, "I already have lots of brothers".

But he responds, "You will be living with us now, so we are really going to be your brothers". When I ask them if they know my sister Leanne and my brother Robert, they reply, "I heard they are now living with friends of Maman and Papa and they live over two hundred miles from here."

That is the extent of the information they can give me. I am so surprised since I thought I would be reunited with them immediately.

My foster Maman is very petite, has short reddish hair, piercing blue eyes, always dresses to perfection and very serious but sophisticated.

My two foster brothers, John and Ron are slightly distant and wary at first and I get the impression they were hesitant in having to share their home with a little girl. Although they may have been informed of my staying with them, they do not appear to understand why their parents wanted a pesky little girl living in their home.

The home they live in is in a town called Trois Riviere and the house is very small with only two bedrooms. I am taken to a bedroom which has bunk beds, and a small cot, with one large dresser and the other one is very small, white with only two drawers. This is the room I will share with the boys and I now understand why they were slightly upset. They had to add a cot for me, and the room appears crammed with hardly any extra space. The boys look at me and Ron says, "Look, we have made room for you, and this is your cot. Since you will be staying with us for a while in this room, we want you to feel welcome." Once they become accustomed and accept the fact that I will be part of their family, they are friendlier, and seem to go out of their way to make me feel at ease, such as help me make my bed, and talk to me when I appear somewhat sad and lonely, and we soon become friends.

The remainder of the home has been made comfortable, well decorated with the rooms painted with soft colors, few family pictures, but without any extra flair.

Since space is limited, the house has a basement, which is used as a storage area and the entrance to this basement is through a trap door located in the living room floor.

I have been living with this new family for approximately two weeks and Maman needs to go to the basement. She opens the trap door in the living room and says to me, "Come here, Aileen, I want you to keep this door up for me; I need to get some things from the basement." I do as she asks, put both my hands on the door and try very hard to hold it up. She goes down the steps and I hear stuff being moved around in the basement. The door I am holding is approximately four by four feet in diameter, made of wood and it is real heavy and hard for me to hold it up.

Well, as it happens, I struggle to keep the door up and steady, while standing up, but the door slowly slips out of my hands and it falls just as Maman has started coming up the steps, hitting her on the top of her head. There is no bleeding but she gets a large head bruise. I am only four and I just could not hold the door up any longer. I am so surprised that it hits Maman; I do not realize that she had started to come up the steps and am not thinking of the consequences if I let go of the door. I do not even think that it will hit Maman.

She is so angry at me and starts shouting, "Did you not see me on the stairs and if so, why did you drop the door? How could you do this to me; I think you did this on purpose, I know you're angry because we took you away from your family at the orphanage, but you should be thankful that we are providing a home for you. You're going to be disciplined for deliberately pushing the door on me; you are such a stupid child." She now proceeds to beat me with a strap, all the while shouting, "You did this on purpose, and so far you have done nothing right in this house, you are so clumsy" and she continues with her beating. After the beating, she makes me sit on a kitchen chair and says, "You will sit here until you stop your crying".

I have never been yelled at like that before, nor have I received beatings at the orphanage and I am so upset at being treated this way, plus the strap really hurts. I want to go back to be with my brothers and sisters, they always took care of me. I do not feel that I did anything wrong, since the door was so heavy, I could not hold it up any longer.

There is no electricity in this house therefore we use oil lamps for our lighting. These lamps have a glass base for the kerosene with a wick going from the base to the upper glass globe. One evening Maman mistakenly pours gasoline into the base

instead of kerosene and as she lights the lamp, it
instantly becomes entirely engulfed in flames.
Without any regard for her safety, Maman rushes
outside with the fiery lamp and throws it in the
creek adjacent to the house, thereby avoiding an
explosion and fire within the home. She is hailed
as a hero by the town's people. She speaks softly
with neighbors and is very well liked and
admired; no one is aware of how Maman
disciplines with a loud stern voice, which I have
only heard her use in her own home. If I do not
respond to her demands immediately, she is prone
to use whatever objects she has in her hand or
anything which is readily available to administer
punishments. This might be a leather strap, or
whipping stick. She hits me on the body,
primarily my back and shoulders, with a lot of
yelling about my disobedience, my slowness and
awkwardness at following her instructions.

Papa is the foreman of the sawmill; both Papa
and Maman are well respected and no one in this
small town suspects the turmoil and upheaval that
takes place with their foster child in their home.

One month after moving in with this family, I
get myself into trouble. I have to go to the
bathroom and I wait too long, so I rush to the
bathroom, only to find out it's being occupied. I
stand at the door, asking to be let in, but Papa,
who is in the bathroom, tells me to wait. I wait
and I wait until I just can't wait any longer and
finally soil my pants. When Papa comes out of the

bathroom and sees what I did, he yells for Maman, and says, "Look at this; the child just dirtied her pants, do something about that and make sure she does not do this again". Maman takes one look at me, yanks me by the arm and pushes me in the bathroom and says "take off all of your clothes;" I do as she asks and when I have nothing on, she starts to beat me on the back with a stick, all the while screaming, "you stupid child, can't you ever do anything right".

A few days later, I wake up in the morning and find my cot all wet. I am so embarrassed since I realize that I wet the bed. How am I going tell Maman? When I finally get up the courage and tell her, she gets very angry and tells me to remove the sheets from the bed and take them to the washing area, but I know from the way she glares at me that I will be receiving a beating for this incident. When I return to my room, after taking the sheets away, here she is waiting for me. She gives me a beating, all the while screaming at me, "You did this deliberately, you are so stupid and an undeserving child, you have no manners and it seems you try to make more work for me". She beats me so hard with her leather strap that I just lay on the floor and cannot stop my crying, so she finally walks away. From that time on, when I go to bed, I lie on my cot and try to stay awake, to be certain I don't wet the bed again.

As time goes by, I keep waiting and waiting to be reunited with Leanne and Robert, dreaming of when I will be able see them. One day I ask Maman "where is Leanne and how can I go to see her?"

Maman responds, "We don't have time to go right now, Papa has to go to work, but maybe we can go in a few months."

After a few months of living with this family, they receive word of a new job opening for a much larger saw mill and Papa decides to apply for the job. He is fortunate to be accepted and they decide to move to this new town called Rapid Sept, which is located at the northern tip of Quebec. This is another lumber town approximately a hundred miles further North, and Papa has already purchased a house and immediately made arrangements to renovate to his specifications.

Our new home had previously been a simple log cabin and although the exterior of the house appears to have retained the appearance of a log cabin, the additions made to the home are clearly visible from the exterior, even though they are also made of logs. The house is situated on a large piece of land, close to the river, overlooking the waterfall and rapids. The interior has been completely renovated and upgraded to a beautiful comfortable home. The walls in the living room area as well as the dining room are painted beige, and the kitchen a soft yellow. Maman decorated the home with beautiful pictures in all the bedrooms, depicting sceneries of snowcapped mountains, as well as pictures of brown bears, which are feared in this area. The kitchen is very large and modern, equipped with a stove operated by gas, with two ovens, making it much more convenient for Maman since she loves to bake all of our pastries and bread. We have a huge icebox to handle a large block of ice, which is delivered once a week and have electricity for lighting only, throughout the house. There is a separate dining room that can accommodate at least eight people comfortably; three bedrooms, and a beautiful living room with a large window overlooking the waterfalls.

The entire town is surrounded by the river, rapids, two large waterfalls, and an electrical plant adjacent to the lumber mill by the river. In any normal circumstances, this would have been a very pleasant and ideal place to grow up. The area appears so serene and calming, specifically hearing the sound of the rapids and waterfall. The townspeople all know each other and it seems very pleasant. The autumn season is a sight to behold. The deep forest turns gold, yellow and bright orange and the vivid colors are spectacular.

I have my own room, which has been decorated in pink, with a bedspread of blue and pink flowers. Scenic pictures depicting lakes and snow, hang on the walls. This is the most beautiful room I have ever seen. There are also books of fairy tales, such as Cinderella, Pinochio, Rhumpleskin and Snow White. Small figurines of children are situated on the dresser, and I just cannot believe I have such a pretty room. I am very concerned about making a mess because I know all of this can be taken away from me therefore I am very cautious so as not to break anything. I know that eventually I will learn to relax, because I really want to stay in this room. I am usually sent to my room after the many physical beatings I receive along with the verbal screaming about my awkwardness and inability to do anything right. I am forced to stay in this room for hours on end, perhaps from four to five hours at a time. Unknown to Maman I find peace and solitude in this room, spend many hours daydreaming, napping, or looking at the pictures and attempting to reread my story books. My favorite book is Rumplestinskin, but I also like Snow White, and sometimes compare Maman to the wicked witch. No one in the household is fully aware that I prefer the solitude of my bedroom to any of the other rooms in this new house, while I am home from school. If Maman had any idea of how I felt about this room, she would remove all the books, or she would insist I remain in the dining or living room along with rest of the family. I miss a few dinners because of discipline; and it never bothers me. I wonder if I might be doing things deliberately just so I can spend more time in my room for the peace and solitude I so need.

Every day Maman tells me, "You have many siblings at the orphanage and I so wish I could return you to this orphanage".

I do not understand why I was taken away from the orphanage in the first place or why Maman wanted another child. Actually all I want is to be sent back to the orphanage so I can be reunited with my family again. Every time she threatens to send me back, I include a wish in my nightly prayers that she will follow through with her threat and allow me to return so I can be reunited with my brothers and sisters. I miss them so much. There has been absolutely no contact from any of my siblings since leaving the orphanage. I am still waiting to see Leanne and Robert and ask, "Maman, where are Leanne and Robert, when can we see them?" But she refuses to reply to my questions. This new home does not appear to have any warmth or love. I do not remember seeing any affection shown toward John nor Ron.

In this small town, the only highlight of the week is attending church on Sunday. The entire town is Catholic and we attend Mass every Sunday; after Mass, all the people gather on the church ground and visit. Although I would like to join my schoolmates for some fun, I am forced to stay with Maman. I do remember a new English speaking family moving into town and once it was determined they were Protestant, the entire town refused to extend them any welcome. They were the topic of discussion on Sunday mornings, after Church service, and everyone appeared to heave a sigh of relief when they were obliged to leave town, due to being unable of obtaining a job at the sawmill. The town had a party to celebrate their departure.

Papa is holding a foreman's position at the sawmill and since the mill employs numerous lumbermen, it takes much more of his time to handle the management and he is seldom home until late in the evenings. Therefore all the running of the household is handled by Maman.

She is an excellent homemaker, keeps the house spotless and is an outstanding cook. Maman has a weekly schedule which is seldom deviated, such as Monday is washing clothes; Tuesday, ironing; Wednesday, mending; Thursday; house cleaning; Friday; baking; Saturday; grocery shopping and Sunday is a non-working day, except for cooking family Supper. I have light duties, such as dusting the furniture and baseboards, as well as sweeping, which I do not mind doing, as a matter of fact, I enjoy the chores, hoping that these will please Maman. They say that whatever you learn as a toddler and pre-teen years, you are apt to retain and use in later years. If nothing else, I become accustomed and learn neatness under Maman's rules. Also, I am never allowed to show anger nor frustration, if I do so, it is a reason for another beating; therefore I have trained myself to hide my frustrations and seldom show anger. This has stayed with me, and to this day, I can remember very few instances in which I have yelled or shouted in anger.

I do want to interject that there are some good things happening as well. After a couple of years living with this family, we are now finally taking a trip to Rouen, to visit the other foster family who has taken in Leanne and Robert and I can't wait to see them. The distance is approximately two hundred miles and to me it seems that the drive is taking forever.

When we finally arrive, and I am able to get out of the car, I see both Leanne and Robert run towards me, then give me the biggest hug, all the while crying tears of joy at being reunited. We had been apart for over two years; therefore we had a lot of catching up to do. The first night there, I share a room with Leanne. It is pure delight to be reunited. I am having so much fun for once and we can't seem to get enough time to visit, we talk and play, stay up late and wake up real early so we can spend more time together and it seem like we have never been apart. The visit is for just a few days. The morning we are supposed to leave, Ma Tante, Leanne's foster mother says "Leanne and Robert will be leaving tomorrow to attend a week at a summer camp not far from here and it might be a good idea for Aileen to join them at the camp. When they return from camp, we can bring her back to you, which will give us a small vacation and we can see your new home".

After much deliberation by Maman and Papa, they agree to allow me to stay another week. I am so elated and cannot believe that I will be away from Maman for at least a week. I really look forward to this new adventure, as well as spending more time with my brother and sister. The next day Leanne, Robert and I join a whole group of children and take the bus ride to the mountains. The bus is filled with children our own age, and it is a fantastic ride. The campsite is situated near the snowcapped mountain, overlooking a beautiful lake. The entire week at camp is pure joy, we hike, canoe on the lake and sit by the fire in the evenings listening to various stories told to us by the camp counselors, play games; we have numerous sing along with friends sitting by the campfire in the evenings. I share a tent with my sister and this is by far the most enjoyable time since leaving the orphanage. We return from the camping trip and the following day we all take off again for the trip to Rapid Sept to rejoin my foster family, which gives me another opportunity to spend more time with Leanne and Robert. On this return trip I notice how their foster parents treat my siblings and cannot understand the difference in families. They all appear to love each other and treat one another with understanding and respect. I am desolate when they leave to return to their home, I cry and cry until Maman threatens to give me a spanking if I do not stop my sniveling.

CHAPTER 3

DAILY ABUSE

Maman takes great pride in making certain that I look and act like a dainty little girl with my hair in long ringlets on a daily basis, specifically while attending school. Therefore I sleep with large metal hair rollers in my hair every night, which is extremely uncomfortable. Maman is also an excellent seamstress and makes all of my clothes, which consists of beautiful dresses of various colors, trimmed with lace, with matching hair bows for my long hair. Since I am consistently told that I am not pretty, I always feel awkward, even though I am the best dressed girl in the school with my clothes, socks, hair ribbons all matching. Sometimes, I just wish I could be dressed like the other girls so that I don't always have to be concerned about my clothes.

The daily morning ritual, which I so dread, is having the metal curlers removed so that my hair can be combed into ringlets. The combing starts around seven in the morning, and in order to properly do this, I am instructed to stand at attention with Maman standing behind me. There is absolutely no consideration from her. When she yanks off the metal rollers out she consistently pulls my hair without any gentleness; however, if I fidget, or move my head, she yells at me, "You are such a clumsy child, hold still so I can try to make you as pretty as possible, however you are such an ugly and awkward child, it is very difficult to make you pretty, so stay still or you'll receive another spanking". If I move while she combs out my hair, she usually clobbers me across the head with her brush then slams me against the wall. When the combing is complete, my hair is normally in perfect ringlets. To this day, I have a difficult time coping with anyone standing close behind me; I find it uncomfortable and will always attempt to sit with my back close to a wall for a sense of protection

Although I am dressed like a little princess, I never feel pampered, because if I soil my dress or lose a bow out of my hair out comes the famous leather strap and the beatings on my back starts with Maman consistently yelling and screaming, "You are such an ungrateful ugly child; even though I try and try to make you look as pretty as possible, you are still awkward and ugly".

I attempt to be very careful in order to avoid any mishap that could stain my clothes or cause a tear therefore do not join in with classmates at recess, always making excuses, so that I can stay at my desk and not take any chances of messing up my clothes. I am considered a loner and do not have any close friends, and this bothers me, but I know I could never join them after school or invite them to the house. There are many times that I long for friendship, a close girlfriend, one I could reveal secrets to, or perhaps join my classmates in outdoor activities. I feel I am a competitive person, and would love to join in their games, such as racing, hide and seek and I do miss not having friends. As for schoolwork, I generally do not have any problems, since I sit at my desk during recess and work on my lessons.

Unfortunately, I can't help but wonder why I am such a difficult child. I have lost my mother at such a young age, lived at an orphanage for just a few months then I am removed from my brothers and sisters to live with complete strangers. This may be causing me to be rebellious, thus giving Maman many reasons for her harsh treatments. I am consistently reminded of my good fortune in being allowed to live with this family, instead of living at the orphanage and that I should be thankful for the comfort they provide. In my child's mind, I would even give up my favorite room if I could be returned to the orphanage so that I could be reunited with my family. I keep biting my nails and I walk with slumped shoulders, which causes Maman to repeatedly yell at me, "Walk straight, hold up your shoulders and stop biting your nails". I hear those comments daily, but I cannot stop biting my nails.

Maman is a fantastic cook and takes great pride in her cooking. The Sunday meal, which is our family gathering, always consists of roast beef, mashed potatoes, gravy and vegetables and it is always delicious.

Weekly Breakfasts are a nightmare. Maman insists that I eat everything placed on my plate every morning before leaving for school, but after the hair-combing ordeal I have absolutely no appetite. I am so upset I can't possibly eat anything after all that pain and stress. I always feel depressed and nauseous. It drives Maman mad when I don't eat what she has loaded onto my plate, and she lashes out from behind me, striking my shoulders with her whipping stick until I give in and shovel the eggs or porridge into my mouth. The whole process takes so long that I am always late for school and miss the morning prayers. Why didn't I just eat, and avoid the beatings? To this day, I cannot understand my own stubbornness, since I am fully aware of the consequences. I am uncertain as to the reason why I sit there, refusing to eat, is it in order to frustrate Maman, because she considers herself a great cook, or is it just that I have absolutely no appetite?

Since the school is only two blocks away, Maman has me come home for lunch and we go through the same struggle as in the morning, primarily me refusing to eat the vegetables she has put on my plate, Maman becoming furious, insisting I eat everything and again I am late for the afternoon session at school, missing the prayers. Although Maman is an excellent cook, there are some foods that I hate, such as broccoli, peas, cauliflowers and beans, but to Maman there is no such thing as refusing to eat vegetables. I am forced to eat everything put on my plate. I upchuck many times and am subjected to beatings until all the food is eaten, including what has been thrown up. The evening meals do not seem to be a problem, since I am not forced to eat all that has been put on my plate. Maybe Maman does not want Papa or her sons to see a demonstration of her treatments to me. To this day, there are still some of those vegetables, specifically peas, beans and cauliflowers, which I cannot even look at and will not eat. Also I am not allowed to drink any beverage during my meals; even though she always places a glass of milk in front of my plate before I start eating. If I attempt to reach for that glass before my plate is clean, this is cause for yet another hit with the baton. This style of eating was so ingrained in me, that I still cannot take a drink or reach for a glass of water with my meals.

Due to the fact that I miss joining the classes in saying my prayers because of my tardiness, for both mornings and afternoons sessions, I receive the following punishment when I arrive home from school in the afternoons. I am made to kneel in front of the crucifix, which is located on a wall in the dining area, position my arms up, similar to the cross and am instructed to say the "Lord's Prayer" and the "Rosary", which are the two prayers I missed at school. I am forced to go through this ordeal every afternoon, after school. I challenge anyone to attempt to kneel and spread your arms out similar to a cross, with no support for the arms. You will find it very difficult to keep your arms up for more than a five to ten minute period. In my case, when my arms start to sag or drop, after eight to ten minutes, it is cause for another beating while I am kneeling, with the majority of the hits on my head or shoulders. Of course, I sustain cuts on my head which causes bleeding, making a mess on the floor. This makes Maman even angrier and I am forced to clean the mess I have created. Between saying the prayers, the beatings and my emotional state, these episodes seem to last approximately one hour each day. Although I usually end up with numerous bruises, they are seldom visible, since most of the hitting is being done on my body and back. If major bruises are visible, I am usually forced to stay home from school until most of the evidence of beatings have disappeared. This causes me to be absent from school on numerous occasions. I shy away from making friends at school, concerned that other children will find out just how many times I misbehave at home. Her own children, John and Ron attempt to stay out of the way whenever I am being disciplined, either by playing outside or staying at a friend's house. I do not remember any discipline being applied towards the boys.

Only once does Maman completely lose her temper; I am sitting at the table for my breakfast, with her standing behind with her whipping stick, hitting me on the right shoulder in an attempt to get me to eat my porridge which is served lukewarm with no milk nor sugar added. I hate it, and I usually gag when I try to eat it. I jerk around to avoid her next hit and I tap my plate with my elbow, which pushes the plate onto the floor, spilling all the oatmeal, making a complete mess of the kitchen floor. She gets so furious, especially when she moves back and steps on the spilled food causing her to almost lose her footing. She is so furious by that time, that she keeps hitting me with her baton over and over about the head and face numerous times, all the while yelling, "You are such an undeserving child, you almost caused me to fall, you are so clumsy, now you will clean up your mess and I don't want to hear any sniveling or crying from you. Get on your knees right now and clean this up". All through the cleaning up, I keep thinking that she is the one who caused this and I just can't understand her anger at me. Spilling the food was an accident. When I finish wiping up the porridge, I am sent to my room, without any explanation as to why I am not going to school that day. By this time, I start to hurt, so I lay down on the bed and my face, specifically my nose really hurts badly and I cry myself to sleep.

When I am finally allowed out of my bedroom after several hours later, the area surrounding my left eye has turned black and blue and my right eye is really swollen so that it is partially closed. My nose has been bleeding and I have blood caked all over my face; my lips are so swelled up, that I have a difficult time talking. I have suffered two black eyes, facial swelling due to a possible broken nose and cut lips. To this day, I still carry a scar on my upper lip. The shock on her face when she sees me is a surprised look, and then it turns to anger. She makes me wash my face, then sends me back to my room and says, "I want you to stay in your room and don't even think of coming out. You are restricted to your room until tomorrow morning when the boys have left for school; maybe this will teach you to finally eat your food without giving me problems." When I wake up the next day, she says, "Your face is looking horrible, and this is what happens when you really mess up. You will be staying home for a few days at least until you feel better." It is unfortunate that the only time she speaks to me in a normal tone is when she becomes concerned about my appearance.

As I stay home and the healing seems to take more time than she has anticipated, she again gets so angry, especially when she realizes how long it will take for the bruising to disappear. I am instructed to stay in my room most of the time, especially when the boys or Papa are home. Although I really enjoy staying in my room, I can't wait to go back to school and have a break from this wretched house. When a week has gone by and the bruising is still very evident, she forces me to apply heat to my black eyes with hot cloths, in attempts to reduce the swelling and the dark colors. She merely shows her frustration by ignoring me, and if she talks to me it is with anger. I stay home at least twelve to fourteen days, which forces her to stay with me and also restricts her from going on her errands. She does not appear to be overly concerned about the injuries, as much as what the neighbors will say if they see my condition. Although Papa has seen me when the bruises are clearly evident, it does not appear that he cares and no comments are made in my presence. The black and blue has finally disappeared and I am at last allowed to return to school. Although my face appears to be normal again, my cut lip leaves a scar, which is still slightly evident to this day.

CHAPTER 4

WINTER FESTIVAL

The one enjoyable winter event I do remember while living with this family, is the annual Maple Festival in mid-winter. The entire town participates on this "Maple Festival" day and all townspeople travel by horse and buggy to the forest, which is within a short distance of the sawmill, and rapids. The preparations include tubes which have to be inserted into the trunks of the maple trees with pails hanging under the tubes to collect the sap from the early morning on; as well as the gathering of wood for the large fire to be built under the large kettle which will be holding the sap, once it is obtained from the trees. The sap is then poured into this huge round kettle which hangs over the outdoor fire, and allowed to reach a boiling point; then the fire is reduced so as to allow the sap to simmer. All the children gather around the fire, singing songs while we are waiting for the sap to boil. Once the sap turns to syrup, it is poured onto fresh snow, so that we can make our "MAPLE snow cone". That is by far a real fun day for the entire town and my highlight of the winter season, because this is the only time that I am allowed to play with schoolmates, outside of the schoolyard. Although Maman visits with neighbors after church, I cannot remember visiting friends or neighbors at other times or neighbors visiting us, except once.

CHAPTER 5

VISIT FROM FATHER

I have lived with this family for approximately four years when my father makes an appearance. He arrives unannounced introduces himself, and I have absolutely no idea who he is. He is invited in by Papa, and then approaches me and tries to give me a hug. Since I do not know him, I back away and that is when he says, "Hello Aileen, I am your father". I still do not recognize him, but allow him to give me a hug. He is very thin, is not tall, wears a beard and is dressed in work pants with a heavy sweater. He appears much older than I remembered him. I have absolutely no idea where he is living, and if he is working. He appears to be a complete stranger to me. I certainly have no feelings for him and am very shy around him.

He takes me for a walk around the vegetable garden which has a walkway surrounding the area and he attempts to have a conversation with me, but since he is like a complete stranger to me, I do not feel comfortable opening up to him. He has a brisk voice and he asks me, "Are you well and do you like your new home?" Before he gives me the opportunity to answer he says, "You look very nice and appear to be very well taken care of, I think this is the best place for you to be." Since I am so shy around him I do not feel comfortable enough to tell him how bad my life is at this home, nor do I want him to know of my poor behavior which is the cause of the severe beatings I am receiving, I do not respond to his comments, and he surmises that my silence is my way of agreeing with him and he drops any further inquiry. I am also fearful he will tell Maman of my complaints and also worried about what he will think of me if I complain, so I am very subdued. He has already been shown my deluxe bedroom and I am certain he notices the way I am dressed with the fancy hair, dress, bows etc. He appears to be satisfied that I am in a very good home and he leaves with no further inquiry, no hug nor love shown. When he leaves, after a visit consisting of just a few hours, I do not have any feelings towards him, since he appears so cold and uncaring.

CHAPTER 6

EXTREME PUNISHMENT

One of the punishments that I receive from Maman is so drastic that I had repressed the memory of this mishap until approximately twenty years ago (I am now in my seventy's). I vaguely remember what I may have done to have caused her to impose such a harsh discipline. The school teacher may have given a note to my foster brothers to deliver to Maman regarding my delay in handing in a written assignment involving geography. I had completely forgotten to do the assignment as I found this subject very difficult. Maman is very strict with school work, very proud and insistent that we excel in school.

I arrive home from school, around four o'clock in the afternoon. While I am taking off my outdoor clothes, Maman stomps into the hallway very upset, yelling at me about how irresponsible I have become. The more she talks, the angrier she gets. She then says, "When you have put your clothes away, return to the kitchen for your prayers."

I murmur to myself, "I don't want to kneel and say prayers". She hears me and that is when she totally loses it; she gets so angry she suddenly opens the front door and kicks me out of the house. It is midwinter, with subzero temperatures dropping and night is rapidly approaching. She refuses to allow me back into the house. I am not wearing proper winter attire such as mittens, snow boots or even a jacket and I am forced to stay out for what I believe may have been up to six hours. Although I pound on the door, crying and begging to be allowed back inside, there is absolutely no response and the door has been locked, so there is no way I can enter. I realize now that I could have gone to a neighbor for help, but that would have meant admitting that I had misbehaved and I am too proud to admit to wrongdoings. After a few hours, I finally get so tired that I do not have the energy to continue to beg, or cry and since I realize that all will be to no avail anyway, I finally sit down on the porch steps, trying to decide on what to do next; I note the soft snow, and am so tired that eventually I step down from the steps and lay down in the snow. I either fall asleep or get so cold that I pass out due to the severe cold. I wake up from unconsciousness to find myself sitting on a kitchen chair, propped up against the table, with my feet in lukewarm water in a bowl on the floor; my hands in a bowl on the table also with lukewarm water and with blankets around me. Both Maman and Papa are sitting across from me at the table and for once, Maman appears troubled and very concerned. Hot chocolate has been made and once I finally come out of my daze I am instructed to drink the hot chocolate placed in front of me so that it can help to warm me up. It is around ten o'clock at night. I am shivering, crying, and oh so cold. It takes me several hours until I start to get warm with the help of hot chocolate, but my hands and feet are so hurtful with sharp pains. The hot chocolate seems to be the best medicine to warm my body but it does not help my hands and feet. A few days later my feet and hands start peeling and this goes on for at least a week.

Again, I am being kept out of school for at least two to three days allowing me to recuperate from this disaster. I was fortunate that Papa came home from work, when he did; I can only assume that when foster Papa arrived around eight or nine o'clock in the evening, he found me passed out in the snow. Had he not come at that time, I may not have survived this punishment. Her abuse of me is not only physical; it is also emotional. She consistently informs me, "You are so clumsy, awkward, and will never be beautiful. I keep trying to make you into a good little girl, but you are so disobedient, awkward and ugly, it is impossible to change your attitude. I don't know if you will ever develop to be a pretty girl." Then, she repeatedly says, "Your father did not care for you, he only visited you once and couldn't wait to leave, which shows that he realized just on how bad you are. Also your family certainly does not want you since they have never tried to contact you. It's sad however understandable that nobody wants you around due to your behavior and personality". The more I hear of those failures, the deeper I sink into low self-esteem.

CHAPTER 7

CHRISTMAS

I remain with this foster family close to six long years and endure everything Maman dishes out to me. I do not remember ever celebrating a birthday; nor do I remember any birthday celebrations for their two sons. I remember reading about young children being tucked in bed and being read stories, but since this has never happened to me, I think these events happens only in fairy tales. Even at my young age, I become an avid reader and find peace and solitude in my fairytale books.

At Christmas, the usual ritual is that the entire family attends Midnight Mass, return home and open whatever gifts are under the tree, then have a midnight breakfast, eating the French Canadian meat pies, known as Tourtiere. The midnight breakfast is a custom of the French Canadian and children are allowed to play with their toys until all hours of the night. Usually I am never included in the opening of gifts ritual, nor allowed to join in the midnight breakfast, but am sent to my room upon returning from Mass while the remainder of the family continues with Christmas celebration. I usually dress for bed, perhaps reread one of my precious books, and eventually fall asleep.

At the age of eight, on this one specific Christmas Eve, we return from Midnight Mass with a new family that had just arrived in town. As I start to walk to my room Maman says, "Aileen, where are you going, it's time to have our Christmas celebration, so come on and join." At first I am amazed that she is talking to me. This is the very first time I am finally allowed to join the family and guests for the Christmas meal, or even allowed to participate in the gift exchange, since there has never been a gift for me. I am very hesitant at going forward into the Christmas room, and I am thinking I have not heard Maman correctly, however much to my surprise when everyone goes to the Christmas tree I am also pushed forward towards the tree, and find that I have a gift, which turns out to be a beautiful box, all wrapped in silver paper. When I open the box, I find the most beautiful doll, with golden curls, all dressed in a pink dress, with lace underwear, sox, shoes, all wrapped in a delicate fancy baby blanket, blue in color with white lace. I have never seen anything so beautiful; I am so delighted that Maman took the time to make these clothes for the doll and I realize that this gift is mine to keep. I am so elated since it is the first and only gift I have ever received while with this family.

Once Christmas breakfast celebration is over, I am finally directed to go to my bed and I happily go, taking my doll with me. I run to my bedroom all the while clutching my doll, get ready for bed, still holding her, making certain that she will be tucked in bed with me. It takes me a while to fall asleep due to my excitement and I just can't take my eyes off my new doll, trying to figure out what name I will call her. The next morning when I wake up, the doll and blanket are both gone. At first I think that the doll is under my blanket and search the entire bed, including under the bed, then I realize that all has been removed. I never see my beautiful doll again. I do not ask where the doll is, concerned that Maman will think I lost her, or damaged her in some way and am hiding her so she can't see what damage I may have caused. I later realize that the entire gift exchange and Christmas celebration for the entire family was just a show for guests to see how the family enjoyed Christmas, and the closeness of the family. I figure this out when one of my schoolmates approaches me after the holidays and says to me "You are so lucky to have a Maman who gives you such beautiful gifts, and is able to sew all of your doll's clothes; it must be wonderful to have such a caring Maman." Since the only time I had a doll given to me was that one on Christmas Eve, I realized that the friends who visited the family told everyone on how fortunate I was to be living with my foster family. I do not ask Maman what happened to the doll because I am concerned this could be cause for yet another beating.

Their two sons are never mean to me, although as boys will do, they tease me constantly, specifically about the fact that I do not belong to the family. Although I do not remember Maman ever showing love or affection to her two sons, I also do not remember her physically abusing her sons. Of course I am so unhappy and wrapped up within my own little world; I could be missing her actions of affection towards her own children. I vaguely remember being allowed to play in the front yard with their sons, but the only toys available for the outdoor, were trucks, or cars, as well as a wagon. Sometimes, the boys would put me in the wagon, pull and all the while sing little songs similar to this, "This is our little sister who can't do anything right, poor, poor little Aileen". These incidents may have occurred on very few occasions. Actually I did not mind the songs, and I enjoyed playing outside and wished this would happen more often.

During, World War II, due to shortage of food, the entire country has been placed on ration and each family have been allowed food coupons for specific items such as sugar, butter and most meat products. One day, Maman was in the middle of baking cookies, realized she did not have adequate supply of sugar, and says to me, "Here is my coupon book, take it and go to the store to get our ration of sugar and do it quickly, since I want to finish these cookies." I run through the town, arrive at the grocery store and request one pound of sugar. As I make my purchase Roger, a friend who and always talks to Maman at church, starts talking to me, and we have a short conversation. After a few moments I suddenly realize that I will be late and I tell the clerk I have to go, run out of the store and rush home, since I have been instructed to do this errand as soon as possible; unfortunately I forget about the coupon book and leave it on the counter at the store.

Later that day, Maman searches for the coupon book and she calls me into the kitchen and asks, "Where is the coupon book?"

I look at her and since I now remember leaving it at the store, I respond, "Maman, I forgot it at the store". She immediately calls the store owner. He had discovered the coupon book and put it away, knowing that Maman would call inquiring about the book. The next day, Maman goes to pick up the book, makes me go with her so that I can thank the manager for being so kind. I am well aware, that after we get back home, I will be punished for my carelessness. I am not wrong, as soon as we arrive home; she says. "You made a serious mistake in leaving this coupon book and just so you will remember not to make this error again, I want you to go outside, and select a strong stick that I can use on you for your discipline." I go outside, look for a usable stick, and of course find one that is small hoping the beating will be lighter with this stick. When she sees what I have selected, she says, "Forget about this stick", Then she proceeds to use her favorite whipping weapon, which is the leather strap and gives me a severe beating, all the while saying, "Now you will remember when I instruct you to do an errand, you will do as I request and you have to take responsibility for your actions". She then sends me to my room. That was the last time Maman entrusted me with the coupon book.

CHAPTER 8

VISIT FROM BROTHER

One of the few highlights of my time while living with this foster family is a visit from my oldest brother, Vick. He is thirteen years older than me.

A soldier appears one early evening, knocks on the door; when Maman opens the door I hear him say, "I am here to see my sister, my name is Vick Charet". He is dressed in a military uniform and everyone is so surprised. I do not know who he is. I totally forgot my previous last name therefore as he introduces himself I do not recognize the name. Finally as he enters, he makes eye contact with me and says, "Bonjour Aileen, do you not know me? I'm your brother". He then approaches me gives me a big hug and I finally realize who he is. I am so awed by him and cannot believe that finally a brother of mine is here. He is tall, wearing his Canadian Army uniform, and after a short chat with Maman and Papa, he is shown my room, and he sits down on my bed, lifts me up to sit beside him, and we proceed to chat.

I ask him "How did you find me".

He replies, "I went to the orphanage, talked to the Mother Superior, who was kind enough to give me your address. I also had the opportunity of visiting with Will, Rose, Joan, and Norm and they are all doing well, very concerned about you and when I told them I would try to visit you, they all send their love". I am so happy I start to cry, but this time they are tears of joy. He puts his arm around me and tells me, "No one has forgotten about you nor Leanne and Robert. If I have time, I will also try to visit Robert and Leanne, and tell them I also saw you and you appear to be very happy". I cannot tell him about what my life is like in this home, since this will also admit that I often misbehave. He then relates what his life is like, and that he is due to leave the country within a very short time. He tells me that he made this trip just to see me. I cannot believe that I am sitting alongside my big brother. I am eight years old, and have been living away from my family for five years, and here I thought that no one remembered me.

I ask him "What is it like in the war".

He answers "Little one, you do not need to know the details, but I will tell you we are on the verge of winning, and I believe the war will be over within the next year, and at that time, I will be back to see you." He then proceeds to tell me what the European countries were like, and how he hated the war.

Because he is the only soldier to ever visit Rapid Sept, the entire town decides to organize a parade for him and by being his little sister; I also receive the royal treatment from everyone. I am so proud of him and feel so important to be allowed to walk alongside of him at this parade. Unfortunately his stay is very short; I am so thrilled to see him and I never mention how my life is with the foster family.

As a matter of fact, to me it seems the abuses I receive may be warranted due to the fact I always cause most of my own problems. I have no explanation as to why I behave the way I do and can only say that, I am a very stubborn child and I so want to be accepted and loved, but do not know what is needed to obtain that sort of attention. Since we never visit neighbors, nor associate with them, I have no way of knowing how other children are treated in their own homes, I assume that the chastising and beatings I experience are the norm with every family.

CHAPTER 9

ESCAPE

I have just turned nine years old, and while attending school, I have made up my mind that it is time for me to join the other students and start playing, enjoy myself and get involved with outside activities during recess; I am tired of staying at my desk while all the other students are having a good time outside. Upon returning to my desk after recess, I discover that I have lost a bow out of my hair. I sit at my desk feeling so awkward and miserable since I am well aware that this will be cause for another beating. First, I chastise myself for being so careless then I finally decide I will not go home for lunch. I seek for a place to hide, and then remember seeing a closet adjacent to the restrooms. When school session breaks for lunch, I enter into the closet, close the door softly and hope that the other students will think I went home and could not return for the afternoon session. I have decided that I definitely cannot return to this home right now. I do not know where I can go, but for this afternoon, I can stay in this closet and dream of being with my family at the orphanage or what it would be like to stay in a home like my sister Leanne and my brother Robert. Their foster parents seemed to be so warm and pleasant and I just wish I could have stayed with them. Also, I dream that it would be so nice if my soldier brother returned so that I could explain what my life is like in this foster home and maybe he could return me to the orphanage. I also talk to Mom, who I know is listening and tell her of my problems and wish she could still be here, or be able to give me advice. I just do not want to ever return to my foster home, and wish there was some way to make that happen. Although the time is very boring in that small closet, I am able to stay without any problems.

I suddenly hear loud noises from the classroom, and note that they belong to some of our neighboring parents who have decided to pick up their children and take them home. I have no idea of the chaos I have created throughout the town. An alarm has gone out that a schoolgirl has gone missing and the townspeople have suspended the school, halted work and are in the process of searching the river, the forest and all surrounding areas searching for me. But in the confusion, no one has thought to search the entire schoolhouse

As time passes I finally do not hear any more noise from the classroom, everything is so quiet. I decide to venture out of the closet, open the door and note that all is dark; it must be around five o'clock in the evening but I decide to remain in the closet for a while longer. I don't want to take a chance of running across a student who may have forgotten his books. Once I have convinced myself that the school is totally empty, except for my teacher, who lives downstairs in her living quarters, I come out of the closet. I know I should have been at home, of course, but if I go home, my foster mother will beat me up. I just don't want to go back to this horrible house, but I have nowhere else to go, what can I do now? I finally realize that I have failed to consider what would happen to me later on, or where I can go. It may be that once the very early morning arrives, I may be able to sneak out and start walking towards the next town. I continue to stay near the closet, sitting on a chair by the door and it's boring, but I fill the time with fantasies of young soldiers who will come and rescue me and take me back to my family, my sisters Rose and Joan, my brothers Will, Vick and Norm.

I finally get tired, and decide that if I lay down on the floor, I can go to sleep then I can figure out what to do in the morning, but first I need to use the bathroom. I do not put on a light, but feel my way around until I find a toilet and when I finish, I flush the toilet. The teacher who has living quarters downstairs, hears the toilet flushing and she rushes upstairs, to the bathroom, looks in the closet and finds me. She is so elated and immediately takes me to her apartment, all the while asking me why I did this. I then tell her that if I go back to my foster home, I will be beaten up again. From the way she looks at me, I know she believes me, and she instructs me to sit down at her kitchen table. She then proceeds to contact the person leading the search for me, informing that I am safe and will be staying with her for the night. She makes me a cheese sandwich and serves it with a glass of milk, and while I am eating, she joins me at the table and gently questions me on the type of treatment I have been receiving from my foster parents. She patiently listens while I tell her why I hid, including the beatings I have consistently been receiving, as well as the reasons for the harsh punishments. At first I am very shy and hesitate telling her because she will probably think I am an impossible child, however she keeps prodding and eventually I open up. She tells me that she is well aware that there is a problem since I am missing way too much school time plus she has noticed many bruises.

I eventually realize she believes me, does not appear to think I am an impossible child, and is going to help me. It feels so great to have someone know that I am not a bad girl all the time. I then proceed to tell her of the episode of being kicked out of the house during freezing weather, without proper attire; she appears to get angry and at first I think she is getting angry at me, but she tells me, "You will stay with me until it is decided how you can be removed from your foster parents, you will stay in my apartment, will not attend school, but I will bring you assignments, which you can complete here during the day. If anyone comes to the door, do not answer. I am certain that once your relatives are notified, a new home will be provided and in the meantime, you can stay with me until a new home is located." She then prepares a bed on the sofa in the living room and makes sure that I am comfortable. I am so tired by that time that I immediately fall asleep feeling very secure. The next morning, Mrs. Peroit makes me breakfast but before she goes to the school area, she makes me promise again, that I will not open the door to anyone. It is so great to be able to eat breakfast without anyone looking over my shoulder and the food she gave me taste great. It also feels so good to be alone, and dream about my new home, hoping that I can either be reunited with my brothers and sisters at the orphanage, or find a new home similar to the one Lillian and Robert have, or even better, to be allowed to join them in their foster home.

The second day that I am in Mrs. Peroit's apartment, as I sit on the sofa, playing with a doll Mrs. Peroit left for me, I hear a knock at the front door. I run to the window to see who is at the door. Ron, my foster brother is standing there, waiting for a response and he remains at the door for a very long time. I am absolutely terrified, sit on the sofa and the longer he stays and keeps knocking, the more I become concerned and so afraid he will try to open the door, so I run to the bedroom, try to find a place to hide, and finally decide to hide in the bedroom closet, close the door very gently, and remain in the closet until I hear Mrs. Piroit call for me. By this time, it is dark; I am so terrified that I have convinced myself that I will be returned to the same home and suffer the consequences for my recent behavior.

I am totally unaware of the attempts that are being made by the local authorities to contact my relatives. I am later informed that they were unable to locate any adult relatives therefore it has been decided by the town authorities that they will send me to a Convent in Northern Quebec in a town named Amos. This convent is also a boarding school. Although there are orphanages within the area, the town authorities made the decision to send me to a proper facility due to my age and the history of abuses; therefore it was arranged for me to attend the Catholic boarding school. I have absolutely no information on how Maman and Papa react to this event.

CHAPTER 10

BOARDING SCHOOL

I am being driven to the boarding school by the town mayor and his family. The school appears to house young girls ranging from ages seven on up. As we approach the convent, I note several nuns waiting at the gated entrance, and as soon as I get out of the car, they all hug me and lead me into the school. We enter the Mother Superior's office along with the other nuns; and Mother Superior looks at me kindly and says, "Aileen it's a pleasure having you here. I am assigning Sister Rose to assist you and familiarize you with the school, as well as acquaint you with our rules, and regulations."

It seems that all the nuns go out of their way to try to do everything possible to make me feel at home; however, I am still very distant, withdrawn and so terrified that I may do or say the wrong thing and be sent back to the foster home. The convent is so foreign to me. The building is on a large piece of land, surrounded by trees, and the total area is entirely fenced with only one gated entrance. The time is approximately 6:00 o'clock in the evening, so I am led to the dining room where a plate of hot food is provided. Although I try to eat, I am so nervous and apprehensive that I have absolutely no appetite and am unable to eat, but also very concerned that I will be disciplined for not eating. Once the Nuns realize that I cannot eat, they pleasantly lead me to the dormitory, which is situated on the top level and consists of many very large rooms with several beds, which reminds me of the orphanage. I am appointed a specific bed and note that the only privacy available is when the curtains surrounding the bed are pulled out. I have had a difficult time falling asleep ever since I wet the bed, and this problem becomes worse at this new school. I have many nightmares and am actually terrified. I am so uncertain of myself and feel so lost. It is difficult to explain on how I have been able to overcome the physical abuses received from Maman, however, what affected me the most were the constant, repeated verbal abuses. This has left me with such a severe lack of confidence and self-respect.

At this new school/convent, I am very concerned that I will not be able to do the proper things, specifically getting up on time and being ready for the morning prayers; therefore I keep my uniform on when I go to bed, so as to be certain I will be prepared and on time to attend Mass in the early mornings. This goes on for six to seven days. Finally Sister Rose gently takes me aside and asks, "Why do you sleep wearing your uniform?"

I look at her and am so surprised and amazed that she knows what I have been doing. I reply, "I don't want to be late in the morning and am afraid that if I have to get dressed after waking up I will be late for the morning chapel prayers".

She gives me a big smile then says, "If that is the case, I will be waking you at the proper time so that you will have adequate time to get dressed."

I then ask her, "How did you find out I slept in my uniform?"

She smiles then responds, "Look at yourself and your uniform, do you not see it all wrinkled?" I then look and realize she is correct, because my uniform is a complete mess. She keeps her word and wakes me up every morning. I finally learn to relax and realize I am being well taken care of and finally feel safe. I am still wary of making friends and mainly keep to myself. Surprisingly my schoolwork is acceptable.

At Christmas, all the other children go home for the Christmas holiday and I am the only child left at the school. As it turns out, it is my first true Christmas celebration. I attend Midnight Mass with the nuns and after the Mass I am lead to the large dining room on the second level, which has a large well decorated Christmas tree, all lit up. I also see several gifts under the tree and much to my surprise; most have my name on them. The nuns sit me near the tree and as they hand me each box, they appear so happy and proud to be able to share their Christmas with me. The gifts include clothes, which I desperately need, since I left all of my clothes at the foster home and they also gave me an easel and a set of paints. After the opening of the gifts, I am led to the dining room table to join the Christmas breakfast. What a wonderful Christmas. I later find out that Maman and Papa had driven to the convent during Christmas holiday in an attempt to convince me to return, however the good Nuns refused to allow them to talk with to me and threatened to call the authorities should they persist on creating any further problems.

CHAPTER 11

NEW FOSTER HOME

In January, the foster parents who took in Leanne and Robert had heard about my predicament came to the convent and convinced the nuns into allowing me to live with them since they already had my brother and sister. I am nine years old, have already lived in four different locations, and now will be moved again into a fifth home.

Again, I find myself being into a strange car, but this time it is with Ma Tante and Mon Oncle. From the onset, I realize that this new move is the best thing that could happen to me. Once I enter their car, and give Ma Tante a huge smile; I do not ask where we are going; in my mind, I know that since I dreamed so much of being reunited with them, my dream has finally come true and I am being taken to their home to be reunited with Leanne and Robert. The new foster parents treat me as one of their own and shower me with loving touch, hugs and tuck me in bed at night; always asking if they can get me anything before I fall asleep. This is a very new experience for me. I am elated to be reunited with my sister and brother. I cannot believe my good luck. I wake up each morning thinking that this is only temporary and will wake up once again with Maman and Papa in that horrible house. After a few weeks, I finally realize that I am now part of a happy family. Although they are not affluent, they have so much love within their home that it is a happy household. Robert is a hockey player and readily gives up his skates for his games, playing as the goalie without skates with the coach's permission, just so I can borrow the skates to join with my sister at the outdoor rink. This is the kind of gentle and loving treatment I receive at this home.

"Ma Tante" makes every effort possible to make me feel accepted as well as trying to bring some joy and fun in my life. She takes Leanne and I to a beauty shop and both of us receive haircuts along with permanents, so here we are both with curly hair, we almost look like twins. I bask in all this attention. MaTante is a very warm person, who is not overly concerned about dress code, although I am always neat, she never disciplines me if I ruffle my dresses or dirty my shoes. She allows me to join her and Leanne whenever she goes shopping, takes us to restaurants, which is a first for me and even introduces me to French fries and hamburgers. She is very understanding, and is making numerous attempts to bring me out of my shell. Mon Oncle works on the railroad and when he comes home, we all are allowed to sit and listen to his stories, which are very funny and he has a way with us that is easy and relaxing. I finally am more talkative however, I will not divulge any information regarding the abuses given by the prior foster home, since I am well aware they are friends with Maman and it is always in the back of my mind that it is possible that I could be returned to my original foster home. Although I have changed schools three times during this one school year, I have no problems scholastically and I feel that I have finally found a loving and caring home I hope and pray that I can stay here.

CHAPTER 12

REUNITE WITH NATURAL FAMILY

Spring arrives and unbeknownst to me, my natural father has finally been located and has been advised of my new living arrangements. However, he has also contacted the prior foster parents, to determine what had happened, and was informed that I had attempted to run away and had been a very problematic and difficult child. He arrives suddenly one evening at my new foster home with another one of my siblings, Rose, a sister six years older than me and he appears extremely angry. The very first words he says to me are, *"Well child, I am now in control of you and you are coming back with me, but just remember there is no way you will ever run away from my home. This is your last stop. You will learn to behave properly and obey my rules"*. Ma Tante and Mon Oncle do not argue with him as to my behavior with Maman and Papa, since they don't know what has really happened with my prior foster parents. The tone of my father's voice, as well as the look on his face makes me realize that his home will be my final stop. The happiness that I have finally found in my new foster home has just gone down the drain.

After a couple days, my father, Rose and I take the train to my final destination. I do not want to leave and cry all the way to the station. I find it so difficult to say goodbye to Ma Tante, Mon Oncle and especially Leanne and Robert. This new move will be my fourth home within eight months. Rose, who is six years older than me, is making every attempt to console me and to get friendly. I eventually calm down and once on the train, I try to maintain my composure. Rose is very pretty, has a pleasant outgoing personality and she is doing her utmost to have a conversation with me. I am very concerned about the anger my father had shown therefore I am very subdued. The train ride is a brand new experience for me; I am fascinated by this mode of travel. As time goes by on the train I am able to get to know my sister again. My father seems to have gotten over his anger quickly and actually is being very kind to me. I am finally relaxing, enjoying my first train ride and begin to get excited about meeting my other siblings.

My first language is French but Ontario is all English and although I am thrilled about being reunited with my natural family, I am also very nervous. It has been several years since I last saw my siblings and I am excited about being reunited with them; although I am also very concerned about not knowing the English language. It is fortunate that my father and siblings are all bilingual. When the train reaches our destination, my brother Norman is at the station awaiting our arrival. As soon as he sees us, he races over gives me such a big hug and says, "Hello little sister, welcome home. You have no idea on how much I have looked forward to seeing you again, and you will love it here." He makes me feel so welcome, that I hope this type of treatment will continue, however I am still very shy and hesitant of saying too much.

We finally arrive and my new home is situated on a 100 acre farm. The story as told to me about the farm is that Dad who was an avid gambler, won the farm through gambling. Once he took control of this farm he was finally able to take in my other siblings, who had been in the orphanage for six years and provide a home for them.

The farm has a large barn, chicken coop and a dilapidated two story house. There are no utilities, therefore oil lamps are being used for our lighting, a wooden stove for cooking and the heater is in the basement with only one heating grill in the main living room. We have to go outside to use the outhouse. Since there is no indoor plumbing, we need to obtain our water from the water pump outside, bring the water in pails, and heat it up using large oval containers over the wooden stove. Rain water is also collected from the rain gutters which pours into large round metal containers at each corner of the house and is used for washing clothes, as well as baths. A scrub board is used to clean the clothes and we wring the water out by hand. Rain or shine, the clothes are hung on an outside line left to dry. Of course, everything has to be ironed. It certainly is a different way of a life and I need to get used to this in a very quick manner, since I am anticipated to participate in some of the chores.

Dad is currently working as a chef for the railway dining cars at the time, along with my brother, Norman. They are usually gone for two to three days at a time, and each time they return home, they bring lots of leftover food from the dining cars. We are very poor and my clothes are hand me down from my sisters, however it does not bother me to wear these; I am just so happy to be part of a united family again and that is the most important thing to me.

The year is 1945, the war is over and my soldier brother, Vick, who I am so pleased to see again also moved to the farm with his wife and two toddlers, Gil who is six months old, and Ray who is two years old. I am fortunate to share a bedroom with two of my sisters and feel lucky to have a bed with blankets. My two sisters, Rose and Joan are six and eight years older than me and they had been in the orphanage together for six years, therefore they are very close and I find myself as the outsider having slight difficulties relating to them. Also since they are teenagers, into the music, movies and actors, their conversations are mainly about boys and the entertainment world, therefore the bedroom I am sharing is adorned with numerous picture posters of actors. At the moment, I find I have absolutely nothing in common with my two sisters, since I have never associated with teenagers, nor have I ever had discussions about boys etc. I am nine years old, and am attempting to fit in with my natural family, which is very foreign to me at the moment. Both Joan and Rose are making numerous attempts to make me open up to them, but since everything is new and I am so concerned as to what they have heard about my prior conduct that I am hesitant in getting involved in any conversation with them. Therefore I remain very quiet and shy for the first few months then I finally open up once I realize that they are trying so hard to please me. I soon become much more relaxed and we really start to get along.

The farm house is two stories which is large enough to accommodate all of us, including my oldest sister Ellen, who is now married with two toddlers, Ive, who is one year old and Celine three years old, also my oldest brother Vick, with his wife and two toddler, as well as Will, Rose, Norman, and Joan. Altogether there are fourteen of us living in this house. It takes me a while to feel comfortable with my new surroundings, including my newly found natural family. After a few weeks of living on the farm, I still have long hair and Joan, who has taken me under her wing and makes sure that I am dressed properly finally gets tired of attempting to comb my hair into ringlets, so one day, she decides to cut my hair and cuts it so short, it looks like a butch. It certainly is easier to maintain and it makes me feel so free. I quickly accept and love the new look.

My three sisters and three brothers work hard to make me feel at home. I arrived with my father in July and my tenth birthday is in September. My entire family decide to surprise me with a party for my birthday. I walk in the dining area for supper and all of my siblings along with Dad are waiting. As soon as I step into the room they all yell, "Surprise", I look around to make certain this is for me and then they sing Happy Birthday. As I look up, they have placed streamers with Happy Birthday Eileen. Wow, what a feeling, this is the very first time my birthday has been celebrated. The very first gift I open up is a beautiful doll. Imagine receiving my first doll that I am allowed to keep at the age of ten. Ellen baked a large cake with my name on it and I am so elated.

One day Ellen walks into the house wearing the most beautiful outfit, and then proceeds to show and model three other new outfits. Dad raves about how great they look on her. It is then that she tells him how she obtained these clothes. She relates that she walked into the clothing store, took several outfits to the dressing room, tried on the clothes, and piled the outfits one over the other, walks out of the dressing room wearing these three separate outfits carrying just one remaining item, paid for that one item, and walks out of the store with entirely three new outfits without paying for them. My father is delighted and applauds her for her ingenuity.

CHAPTER 13

NEW SCHOOL

My first day attending my new school is quite a challenge. It is a small country school located approximately two miles from our home. My brother Will, is in the eighth grade and attends the same school, so we both walk to and from school together for my first year at this school.

First grade through eighth grades are in the same room and there are approximately forty students attending. This is my fourth school in one year and everything appears to be so foreign.

As I enter the schoolroom, with all the kids looking at me, I feel so shy and out of place, I would give anything right now to be able to turn around and go home. Now, you must remember, I cannot speak one word of English, so the teacher has decided to place me with the first graders. I sit at my new desk, look around and find that I am seated with six year old children; I am so embarrassed and would like to just get up and leave. Here I am at age ten, sitting with children six years of age and I am unable to understand one word anyone is saying. Everything appears so foreign to me, but I am determined to cope and learn the English language as quickly as possible. I eventually try to speak English, but I have such a strong French accent, most kids cannot understand me and it becomes very frustrating, but I am not a quitter, so I am determined that within a few months, I will be sitting with my own age group and be able to do my English lessons accordingly.

One schoolmate, whose name I have never forgotten, Lenny, is my age and enjoys going by my desk, while I am sitting in the first graders section; he walks by and calls me several names in English, primarily says to me, "You're such a stupid little French baby" also, "You are a dumb ass" which causes all the children to laugh, specifically the children within his own age group. At recess, I mostly stay by myself and quite a few children pass by me snickering and calling me several names. I feel so alone in this school, but will not give up since I am so determined to learn and eventually fit in. When you are attempting to learn a new language as a child, the very first words you pick up are the name calling and swearing ones. I ask my brother Norman, who I knew I could confide in, the meaning of "dumb ass; and stupid" which are the words I remember being used by this horrid kid and when my brother translates the name calling, I am furious.

The next day I am really prepared for this smart ass kid. When he approaches me and starts taunting me again, I stand up, swing my right arm back and take a good swing forward and hit him with all the strength I have, knocking him down to the floor. Of course the entire schoolroom burst out laughing at this and I feel so good.

The teacher looks on but does not reprimand me for this display. After that day, the teasing slows down and I finally am able to make friends. As a matter of fact, Lenny and I become good friends. Although my brother Will also attend this same school, for unknown reasons, does not show preference towards me, so I am left to fend for myself. I think he feels that if he leaves me on my own, I will learn English much quicker and he is right. Within six weeks, I am being transferred to the ten year old section, since I am now able to read, spell and speak English, perhaps with a heavy French accent, however I understand the language enough to be able to keep up with children within my age group. My most difficult class is composition and spelling. So many English words sound the same, but have different spelling and meaning, and it astounds me that the words similar to rough couldn't be spelled ruff.

One of my school assignments is to memorize and recite a specific poem. I work and work very hard on this project and finally when I think the time is right, I approach the teacher during lunch time, when all the other children are out in the playground. Although I am still hesitant and shy about my French accent I say to the teacher, "would it be possible to recite the poem you asked us to memorize?"

She realizes that I waited for all the children to be outside before approaching her so she responds ," That would be good time for you to do this, since all is quiet here", I now proceed to recite the poem, and when I am finished, she smiles and says, "Good work Aileen, that was excellent", I proceed to leave the classroom, feeling so great; as I am leaving, I look back and she has this big smile on her face and appears so pleased. I am finally relaxing and feel that I have been accepted and made the transition with this school as well as my new home. Although, the children still tease me, due to my accent, I am able to handle it, with no problem and eventually they stop making fun of me. At Christmas I am not included in the school play due to the fact that my heavy French accent prevents me from handling any speaking part. However I am fortunate to have a singing voice and have been selected as the soloist within the choir as well as a choir member. Also, the Canadian scholastic program included a yearly singing competition throughout the Ontario province and since I am fortunate to have a fairly good voice I usually am selected to represent our school at the singing competition as a soloist and also perform in the duet competition along with Lenny. Although I do not win any prizes, I always end within the top three competitors. This program assists children such as me, to face an audience and perhaps develop a sense of confidence and I feel very proud of my one talent.

CHAPTER 14

LIFE ON THE FARM

I have been living with my family for approximately one year, am now ten years old thoroughly enjoying my life on the farm. I attempt to make every animal on the farm my pet and feel such freedom. Everyone joins in my exuberance whenever I am able to make one of the animals a pet. I even made pets of two calves; every evening I go to the fence of the corral, call them and they trot out to me, waiting to be petted. My siblings often tease me regarding all my efforts and attempts to pet every animal; it feels so good to be loved and allowed to be myself with such freedom, allowed to run around the fields, with no harsh physical abuses. I am finally able to be a child who is loved and understood properly. My favorite animal is the family dog; he never seems to leave my side. He is a beautiful collie named "Sport", and I dearly love him. One day, he is missing and I search and search to no avail. When I ask my brother for his help in finding Sport, he says, "Dad took him away and shot him. He is dead". I am so astounded and sad. To this day, I still do not know the reason why my collie had to die, however it made me realize that life on the farm can be very harsh. I am totally lost without my best friend.

During the summer of the same year, my brother Norman is acquainted with a family from the city that needs assistance in providing care for their pet, a little Chihuahua named Noiro, while they travel for the summer. Norman who is well aware that I am lost without Sport, offers to take in their pet for the summer, knowing that I will have a companion for the summer at the farm, which will give me time to get over loosing Sport. This little dog becomes my shadow, and we are together all the time. One of my nightly chores is to bring in the cows from the pasture in the early evenings. I used to have to go to the pasture, get behind the herd and prod the cows on towards the barn. Since Noiro has arrived, he joins me in my duties and assists me in bringing the cows to the barn by nipping them on their lower legs, which causes them to come in from the pasture at a faster pace and I do not even have to go behind them in the pasture to get them to move, all I have to do is stand near the barn and call Noiro. The cows start their journey quickly and enter the barn without me going all the way out. When the summer is over, this little pet returns to his home in the city. The next day, after he leaves I stand at the fence surrounding the pasture, call Noiro, and the cows move quickly toward the barn; however after a few days they realize that Noiro is no longer around and they stopped moving. So I have to return to my standard way of bringing the cows in. (Who says cows are dumb). Also one of my chores is to collect the eggs from the hen house in the mornings. Of course, I make pets of two specific hens, called them Mimi and Melli. One morning my two pets are missing. I pick the eggs, take them into the house, then run back to search for my hens but am unable to find them. That night, at the dinner table, while eating chicken, I say, "Mimi and Melli are missing, does anyone know what happened to them, or have you seen them outside of the chicken pen?" No one says anything, however they all look at each other with smirks and I just don't understand why they're all looking at me that way. It never dawns on me that I am eating chicken.

I must have been a model child, since I do not remember ever getting in trouble or being disciplined. During the summer, Will, Rose and I are hired by a neighboring produce farmer to help with harvesting his crops. The three of us pick produce the entire season, which keeps us occupied and actually it is a lot of fun as well as being able to earn spending money and I am able to spend quality time with Will and Rose. I usually eat more fruit than I pick and enjoy every minute of it. This time period of my childhood era is the best any child can wish.

Christmas Eve arrives, all of my siblings appear to be evasive, and I wonder what is going on but when it is bedtime, we all retire to our rooms. I am surprised and figure no one in this household is celebrating Christmas so I go to bed and fall asleep. Suddenly I hear a loud bell ringing, I jump out of my bed, run out of the room; and the downstairs is all lit up. I rush downstairs and see the most beautiful tree, all decorated with numerous gifts under the tree and Christmas music is playing. It is then that I realize that most of the gifts under the Christmas tree have my name on them, I am in a daze. But not for long, since everyone keeps urging me toward the tree to start opening my gifts. Everyone is very much aware that I am in dire need of warm clothes for the winter, therefore they combined their money and bought gifts which included a beautiful fur lined coat, mittens, snow boots, heavy sweaters, woolen caps as well as flannel pajamas, it is unbelievable that this has been done by the entire family. The smiles and anticipation on their faces when I open each gift is wonderful. It is as if they are trying to make up for the lost years. I cannot believe that my family is so caring. We appear to be a close loving family group. We also have Yves and Celine as toddlers, who also received many toys. What a joyous Christmas, and to me it actually was my first real family Christmas celebration.

I am spending many hours on the farm with my older sister's daughter Celine. She is seven years younger and my sister depends on my help with the children; I babysit both youngsters, Celine and Yve on numerous occasions, and thoroughly enjoy the work, which makes me feel part of the entire family. Soon, Celine and I become inseparable. I also get along very well with my sister, Ellen since I feel I can talk to her about anything. She is popular with all of my siblings as well as Dad.

CHAPTER 15

SEXUAL ABUSE

My two sisters Rose and Joan whom I have been sharing a bedroom with, decide to leave the farm and move into town, hoping to find work. They both immediately find jobs and start working. Rose, who is sixteen obtains a job washing dishes in a restaurant, and is able to find a room and board accommodation in town. Joan who is eighteen obtains a full time job assisting a handicap family and they also provide room and board for her.

Since my two sisters are gone, I am elated to have the bedroom all to myself; it feels so wonderful to have some time alone and to be allowed to decorate the bedroom. I tear down all the pictures of their favorite movie stars, and put in pictures of my cartoons and animals that I like. I have big plans for my newly acquired independence. The first week end that Joan is able to get time off work; she returns to the farm in order to take me to the department store and buys me a complete outfit. What a great sister. Everything is working out so well, and I am finally happy and content on the farm with my own natural family.

I am now eleven years old. Approximately three months after my sisters moved to town, an unthinkable horrible episode occurs. I am sleeping soundly and suddenly waken in the middle of the night with my father lying in bed beside me attempting to fondle my breast. I can smell the alcohol from his breath. I try to move away but to no avail since I am being pushed against the wall. He proceeds to grope between my legs into my private area. I do not know what is happening; I try to move away from him and this is when he tears off my pajama bottom, gets on top of me. I don't understand what is happening, except that he is really hurting me. In my child's mind, I think I am being punished for having done something wrong. After he finishes raping me, he leaves without saying a word, and goes into his own room. I have absolutely no idea what has just happened. All I can remember is him getting on top of me, and the rest of what happened has been partially blocked from my memory. I know that I lay there petrified, and all I can think of is that I must have done something really horrific to be given such a harsh extreme punishment, but I just can't think of what I have done to warrant this type of abuse. I am hurting and in a daze but do not understand what just happened.

I wake up early the next morning, I think back on the event of the night before and decide that I must have had a horrible nightmare, but then I see blood on the sheets and as I attempt to move, I am hurting so bad that I now realize my nightmare may have been for real. I do not fully understand what actually happened. I am so confused. I attempt to wash the blood off the sheets, since I am so concerned that I will be in further trouble for staining the sheets, I try to cover them up so that no one will notice the mess I made. I wait until everyone is gone, then strip the bed, take the sheets outside to the water pump, and eventually get the bloodstains out. I hang out the sheets, and when Ellen notices the sheets on the line, I explain that I spilled my drink and needed to rinse them out. I do not see my father that day. The next day he walks in my room and hands me a beautiful gold watch . I definitely do not know what to make of it. I do not need a watch and do not understand the reason for the gift. I still cannot figure out what happened that night, and hesitate asking him, concerned he will give me a beating for soiling the sheets. From that day forward, I have had insomnia, waking up mostly every morning around two o'clock, and it usually takes me approximately one to two hours to go back to sleep.

My father is very intelligent, as well as devious, cunning and sly. He is well aware that I lack knowledge of his actions, that I am so fearful of abuses and have a total lack of self-confidence due to the foster home's physical and psychological abuses; therefore he knows just how he can play on my fears using them against me with a devised plan. He leaves me alone for a few months after the assault, then one day when we are alone in the house he joins me in the kitchen, asks me for a cup of coffee and then makes me sit down so we can have a private chat.

He then tells me, "I am so sorry for forcing myself on you, but I love you so much, I couldn't help myself." He goes on saying, "You're my baby daughter and I will always take care of you". He tries to hugs me, but I shy away from him, and that is when he gets very serious. He says, "I have something important to tell you, and I don't want you to be upset. When I made love to you, which is what I did the other night, I found out that something horrible must have happened to you while you were living in the first foster home". He then says, "Do you remember your foster Papa touching you and forcing himself on you?"

I said, "No, I don't remember"

He replies, "Then it must have occurred when you were very young, because you have a major problem. Your foster Papa must have attempted to abuse you, and may have torn you up, causing a severe injury, and you did not receive the proper medical attention necessary to take care of the problem". He continues, "The way you are now, you will be unable to have children, and you may have a difficult time having sex when you are older, so no man will ever want to marry you".

I am so surprised and totally devastated to realize that I have been injured so severely and will never be able to have children nor live a normal life. I am eleven years old; do not fully understand what he is talking about, except that I firmly believe no one would ever want to marry me. Whatever confidence I have recently attained has disappeared. I am scared, uncertain again, and very concerned about my injury, however I am so stunned, I do not question the full extent of this problem.

He leaves me alone for a few days, then he approaches me again when I am alone and he sits me down and says, " I have had you in my thoughts constantly about your condition, am very concerned about you and since I have had some experience in medical treatment I have done research and found out what can be done about your existing problem, so don't be too concerned, because I now know exactly what is needed to treat you, so that you can eventually be normal. I will obtain whatever medication is required and I will treat you myself, so that no one will know about this."

By then I am in such a daze in finding out that I may never be a mother nor have a normal life, so I say, "OK Dad, do what needs to be done."

He then informs me, "I will also promise that I will tell no one of your condition and will treat you as needed, so don't worry, eventually you will be fine and will be able to have a family once you get married." He also says, "It is important that you tell no one of this, since once they find out, they will tease you and make you feel like you did when you lived in the foster home, unwanted and unloved". He continues, "Please understand that whatever I do to you, is necessary for your recovery. Now I want you to promise me you will tell no one of your condition or of my treatments."

From the way he acts, he appears so confident that he can take care of this problem himself. I firmly believe he will be able to treat me and am so relieved and happy that he is willing to take the time to treat me. In my mind I think, "I am so fortunate to have such a great caring father".

From that day on, he sexually abused me, using whatever means necessary. I vaguely remember the private touching; however, I cannot and do not want to remember exactly what sexual acts he has performed, since I have blocked out most of the sexual abuse. The thing I remember the most was him entering my bedroom in the morning once my family has left the house. He then joins me on the bed and starts to hug me, and grope me between my legs, he then applies a salve that has a strong pungent odor, then his touch becomes hurtful, and as he is pushing into me he also fondles my breast and says, "Your mother had beautiful breasts, and I know you will develop like her". The remainder of any further actions has been totally blocked from my memory.

As a child, I have absolutely no knowledge of sexual acts and I have no way of knowing if what he does to me is right. I realize that I have nowhere to go and feel stuck in this environment, therefore I endure his so-called treatments and perhaps fool myself in really believing he can cure me of whatever condition has been caused by my first foster parents. At first I am thankful that he is able to take care of my so-called problem, and the alleged called treatments continue on for three years. Once I started allowing him to supposedly treat me, I do not know how to stop him, and I so dread the morning hours. I sometimes sneak away in the mornings, pretending that I have early chores, however when I return home, he is waiting for me, and if no one is around, he insists on giving me his treatment. I do not have enough strength to fight him, and he keeps telling me that these treatments are necessary for proper healing.

As my early adolescence passes I start questioning his actions to myself however, have no one to discuss this matter with, and I am still so hopeful that he will be able to treat me accordingly. I had promised not to tell anyone; I feel so desolate and alone again but am looking forward to the day that I will be normal. My moods and personality have changed to my previous condition, very subdued, slumped shoulders and nail biting. Unfortunately, I cannot discuss this matter with anyone. I have made a promise and I still firmly believe he can cure whatever "condition" I have. The incest continues on and while still fourteen, I finally attempt to talk to my oldest sister Ellen. She is fourteen years older, we get along very well and she depends on me for assistance with the children.

Every Friday afternoon, we work together cleaning the house, as well as spend a lot of time talking; taking breaks while eating toast and have coffee. I feel very comfortable with her and decide to confide with her about my problems.

I finally approach her and say, "I have a problem and need to talk to you, however I need a promise from you that you will tell no one", she nods in agreement and I then say, "My problem is that I may have been seriously injured at the foster home, and if it is not taken care of, I may not be able to have children, however I don't understand what the problem is; Dad is taking care of it, but it seems to take so long, maybe I need to go to a doctor to find out if the treatment I am getting is adequate. What do you think?"

She does not appear surprised and she calmly replies "wait, don't tell anyone, I will have a talk with him, find out what type treatment he is doing and will let you know what you need to do". The next day she approaches me and says, "I talked to Dad and he explained to me how he is treating you, since he seems to think you have a serious problem. I don't have enough medical knowledge to dispute his treatments or if what he is doing is the right thing, but he appears so convinced that he can cure you that I highly recommend you continue with his treatments. He also mentioned to me that you may be going to a different school, when you graduate from the eighth grade".

A few weeks later, the old man informs me, "I have decided to have you attend a boarding school once you graduate from elementary school. It's a combination of a convent and boarding school. I have heard good things about this school, and I want you to have a good education. We need to drive over and be interviewed by the Mother Superior in order to be accepted, so be sure you keep copies of your final grades to bring with you at our meeting." This new school idea, I believe was initiated by Ellen, who may have thought that attending the boarding school would take me away from the old man, at least part of the time. If that is the case, I am very thankful for her help.

Although I have no specific proof, I firmly believe he sexually abused three of my sisters, due to the fact that they all had major psychological problems during their lifetime. My sister, Rose seemed to be the most affected since she was very confused and a deeply depressed person. She did not seek counseling and led a very unhappy life.

CHAPTER 16

TEEN YEARS

Rose and Joan are now dating and come to the farm on many weekends, along with their current boyfriends. The boyfriends are usually heavy beer drinkers, and spend many evenings partying on the farm, enjoying themselves with telling numerous jokes of every nature. My father also participates in the partying by telling his own jokes, which seem very vulgar to me. By the age of thirteen and fourteen, I believe I have heard every four letter word both in English and French. I sometimes hide under the stairwell when they are all partying and listen to their antics.

Also, at the age of fourteen, I decide to go shopping for Christmas. Since my spending money is very limited, I decide to copy my sister Ellen's action and attempt to shoplift for Christmas gifts.

I ask my brother Norman to give me a ride into town, explaining I would like to do some Christmas shopping and if he can wait for me for a couple of hours. He also wants to run some errands therefore this works out very well. I enter the large department store and start looking for items I can take. I spend approximately two hours in the store trying to determine what I can steal for Christmas gifts. I feel that since my sister is so successful in doing this, I can also do it. But when it comes to the actual act, I just cannot get up the courage and finally give up when I realize this is not in me to steal someone else's property. I purchase the items that I can afford, and walk to the cash register and pay for whatever I picked up. As I walk out of the store a gentlemen who is standing outside the store, shows me his security guard identification proving that he is an employee of the store and says, "I want to see what you purchased, as well as look into your parcel and purse". I allow him to do a search, and when he is unable to find anything other than what I had purchased he releases me and informs me that he has been watching me for at least an hour, and was so certain I had taken some items. He congratulates me on my honesty. I walk away feeling so fortunate and lucky that I had not stolen any merchandise. This experience certainly taught me a valuable lesson. I have never considered nor attempted to shop lift after that incident.

The farm is put up for sale, since the family is getting smaller. Rose and Joan are now married, and moved into the city of Toronto; Vick and his family have moved to Quebec; Ellen and her husband built their new house and have just moved; Will found employment in the City of Toronto, and has also moved to Toronto, therefore there are very few family members remaining to assist in running of the farm. Within a few months, the farm sold, Dad along with Norman purchased another piece of property consisting of approximately five acres of land and a small house, all within one mile of a small town named Albertville. Both Dad and Norman invested in the construction of a service station on this property. Norman runs the station and occupies the small house. The Dad has purchased a single wide trailer which he has had installed near the service station and both he and I occupy the trailer, whenever I am not attending the boarding school. Dad had informed the family that he had made a promise to God, and that is if he could sell the original farm, he would purchase a statue for the Church, therefore when the sale of the farm was finalized, he purchased the statue of Joan of Arc, who at that time was a Saint in the eyes of the Catholic Church, and donated it to the church he attended. This also demonstrates his strong religious beliefs

Being alone most of the time with father in the newly acquired trailer is unfortunate since he is finally at liberty to molest me, or as he calls it, giving me a treatment, without the concern of being interrupted.

CHAPTER 17

BOARDING SCHOOL

The time is finally here for me to enter my new school. The convent, which is also a boarding school, is approximately fifty-five miles away from my home. The building is constructed of bricks, five stories high, with rooms for the Nuns, then separate areas for the boarding students accommodating over one hundred students. The living quarters for these students consist of individual bedrooms, which are large enough to be occupied by at least four students per room.

Their scholastic program includes the normal educational teachings, including classical music, theater, and an athletic program. All teachers are Nuns. The grounds include walking paths, tennis courts, fields for field hockey, and areas for racing competitions. This school is situated on a fifty-acre area, which also includes a beautiful park.

I share a bedroom with three other girls my age and we soon become good friends. The only problem with sharing a bedroom, is that I still have insomnia and wake up in the early morning hours at approximately two o'clock and generally stay awake for at least an hour or more without the possibility of getting up and moving around, or be able to turn on a light in order to read during that hour.

However I am doing very well scholastically and love the school. My wardrobe is very limited and my roommates decide they will assist me on the proper attire for young ladies when we are not in uniform, as well as proper sanitary techniques and how to use make up. Although many of the students who are attending this school come from loving normal homes, they consistently complain about the food and the strict regiments, while I personally thrive and am in my glory in these surroundings. I go home for the weekends on limited occasions, and make every attempt to stay at the school whenever possible. Many times, I am the only student left at the school and I thoroughly enjoy these weekends. The nuns keep me busy assisting them with clerical work, or library listings and since I am an avid reader, it also gives me the opportunity to lose myself in books. All the students wear uniforms and I feel so comfortable wearing these, since I know I would not have been able to compete with the other students on clothes. Numerous students complain over the accommodations, uniforms and the type of meals served, but for me, this is perfect.

While at the boarding school, Rose and her husband, who live approximately fifteen miles from my school, often come and pick me up on weekends. I spend some quality time with her family. Joan, is living in Toronto, is also married and has three children. She also welcomes me whenever I am able to visit. I realize that the nuns need personal time periodically, so I have to be away from the school for at least two weekends per month. I occasionally go to my roommates' homes whenever possible or attempt to visit my sisters. Otherwise I have to go home and suffer the sexual abuses. I hate those weekends and feel so desolate that my condition has not been cured. Unfortunately, I cannot reciprocate and invite my friends to my home; I am too concerned what could happen with my father.

I am now fifteen and my father becomes ill with bleeding ulcers during the Christmas holidays therefore I am left to take care of him. My Christian teaching teaches me to "honor thy parents" however I definitely have some strong negative feelings about having to take care of him. I feel so guilty having so much animosity and hatred against my own parent, who I am told is attempting to treat my so called condition, and I know I should be grateful to him, but I find it very difficult.

The boarding school grounds have a beautiful creek on campus. The school has a library of various subjects; therefore on the weekends that I remain at the school, I usually sit alone, reading my books for hours by the creek finding solace and calm in the sound of the rippling waters. This, I believe assists me in coping with the abuses. In the evenings, during school weeks, we have study hour from seven o'clock to nine o'clock. After I finish my homework and since I am not allowed to leave the study hall, I usually sit at my desk and read novels, however pretend to do school work by placing numerous papers on my desk, so that the nuns do not see the novel that I am reading, however later on, I find out they were well aware of my antics, but since my grades are well above average, they allow me to think I am fooling them, and continue to let me read my books.

I realize that most young ladies of fifteen, in this current era, are very knowledgeable in sex, due to the advanced education either from school or parents. However in the mid 1950's there is no such thing as sex education in the schools and although I room with girls my own age; I am way too embarrassed to even ask questions on sex. It would have been of great assistance if I had had someone to talk to about these important issues; however we are in a Catholic school in which such subjects are never mentioned.

The Academy believes that their students should have the opportunity to learn all aspect of life, including the arts; they have a glee club, which enjoys a very good reputation and travel giving concerts. I am so fortunate and happy to be one of the lead singers in this choir. The school also puts on a play every year and I am usually selected as a soloist. This definitely elevates my self-esteem, which is the one time I can feel good about myself. The first time I am scheduled to be alone onstage for my solo, I am so nervous. One of the nuns takes me aside after I finished my very first song and tells me she will coach me; give me advice on how to relax once on stage. Her suggestions assisted me greatly, since I have had major problems with self-confidence. It is a wonderful school, with teachers who take personal interest in their students, and attempt to bring out the best of whatever talent they have whether scholastic and or artistic. I am also fortunate to be able to join the group selected to attend an opera in the city of Toronto. What a spectacular evening for all participants. This also taught me to appreciate classical music.

CHAPTER 18

MEDICAL EXAMINATION

I am now fifteen years old and I decide to schedule an appointment with a doctor located in the same town where the boarding school is situated. I am having numerous doubts as to my deformities, and need to determine the exact problems, as well as whether the treatments I am receiving from my father will take care of this condition. I locate a doctor through the telephone book, call and attempt to make an appointment. As I answer the questions posed by the office attendant, she informs me that a guardian or a parent must be present during the examination since I am under sixteen. The week I turn sixteen, I again call this same general practitioner and schedule my appointment giving the purpose of the medical examination is to obtain the necessary medical clearance for me to compete in an upcoming racing event that I wish to participate representing my school, and I also request the examination to include a vaginal examination informing the nurse that I believe I may have developed a vaginal infection. I schedule my appointment for the following Saturday morning.

As I enter the doctor's office, I am so apprehensive and hesitant, since I do not remember ever being treated by a doctor. I enter the examination room, and am given a gown by the nurse, who instructs me to disrobe, put on the gown and lay down on the examination table. The room is completely white, with a few pictures on the wall depicting bone fractures; the examination table has a contraption at the end, which looks like spurs. I get up on the table and sit on the side awaiting the doctor.

When the doctor enters, he takes a good look at me, specifically my size and stomach, which gives me the opinion he thinks I am pregnant. I am five feet two, and weigh approximately 100 pounds. He checks my glands, temperature then instructs me to lie on my back on the examination table and to place both my feet on the spurs, he then proceeds with the pelvic examination. I am so embarrassed with this type of examination, and have a difficult time relaxing, so the doctor keeps reminding me to take deep breaths so that I can feel more at ease, and since I am very determined to find out full details of my existing condition I am willing to undergo any uncomfortable situation in order to obtain a diagnosis.

The Doctor completes the physical examination, looks at me with a smile and says, "_Young lady, you are fine_", _I can find absolutely nothing wrong with you. You have my full approval to participate in any athletic event you wish. As for an infection, there is absolutely_ *no indication that there is a problem, you are in good health.* I sit there for a moment in a stupor, and the doctor says, "Is there is a problem, or do you need to discuss anything further?"

I respond, "No Doctor however, I would appreciate being provided with a note specifying that I am in good physical condition and do not require medication or treatments of any kind". He proceeds to write the note, as requested and I depart from his office.

I ride the bus back to the boarding school in total shock. I feel so dejected and a complete idiot for having allowed my own father to supposedly treat me for an alleged "condition", which was merely a ruse to sexually abuse me for all those years. I cannot believe a father would do that to his own child, or to any child, however I also chastise myself for having been so naïve and trusting, and for not asking him specific questions on what he meant by me having a condition. I am embarrassed and angry to think this was done to me by my own father, who knew of my sensitivities and lack of confidence due to my prior physical and psychological abuses, thereby taking advantage and using me for his selfish needs. I believe sex abuse to a child is the most demoralizing type of abuse. Yet, at the same time, I am elated to discover that there is absolutely nothing wrong with me.

It is impossible to fully explain the feelings associated with incest. There is the embarrassment, hurt, shame and all the negative feelings associated with rape and sexual abuse. These are intensified by knowing that I have willingly allowed this to go on from the time I was eleven years old up to sixteen years of age. I have difficulties in thinking I have been that naïve. It's as if I was complicit in his behavior and the shame will always remain with me. Whatever self-esteem I have attained due to my artistic talent with my singing has deteriorated to the lowest level ever and I am in a world of my own, with all the guilt associated with incest.

Once I return to the school, I take off on a walk and sit by the running creek, hear the rippling water, which assists me in relaxation. As I sit there, I ponder how to handle the situation at home and how to stop my father from allegedly treating this fake condition. I know I cannot report his actions to the local police department. We live in a small town in which they have a small police department and all the police officers are friendly with my family, specifically my old man. They even joined his monthly rolling dice gambling sessions, so I seriously doubt that they will believe me, they will merely look at me and wonder how I could be so dumb or that perhaps I may have been the aggressor in the first place.

CHAPTER 19

CONSULTATION

Coincidentally, a retreat is scheduled for the students at the boarding school within the next two weeks. This retreat consists of attending numerous lectures on scriptures and life in general. These lectures are normally presented by a priest who is well qualified in these types of sermons to young ladies. After much consideration I decide to take this opportunity to request a meeting with Father Flynn, who is the priest assigned to the school, since I am well aware his time is limited at the convent. He will move on once the retreat is over and I will probably never see him again.

As I sit in the office, waiting for my appointment, I am very apprehensive and nervous about what I need to discuss and afraid of the consequences. I enter his meeting room, and I say, "Father, I have a serious problem and I am seeking advice on how to handle the situation".

He takes a good look at me and states, "Young lady, whatever problem you have, I will attempt to assist you in finding a solution, so please take a seat, take a deep breath, and talk to me. You appear very nervous, so let's have a cup of tea and relax. He calls his assistant and request two cups of tea. While we are waiting for our tea, we make small conversation and he attempts to put me at ease. When tea is served, he says, "Let's talk, please feel free to tell me your reason for this meeting, and be assured that whatever we discuss will be confidential." I then proceed as follows: "I started to live with my natural father at the age of 10; when I turned eleven years old, he convinced me, after he raped me, that I had a serious sexual medical problem, due to previous sexual abuses I received at a foster home, however he assured me he had some medical knowledge and he would be able to take care of this problem, if I allowed him to treat me." I then proceed to tell him, "The alleged treatments are still continuing, but I have just found out after obtaining a medical examination, that I do not have any type of problems, therefore my father has duped me into allowing him to sexually abuse me all these years. I also want to inform you that my father alleges strong religious belief and never misses Mass on Sunday, all the while sexually abusing me. Father, I need your advice on how to put a stop to his so called treatments. I have nowhere to go; I do not want to be sent to a foster home again, since I have had a horrific experience as a child with the foster system, so how can I make my father stop the sexual abuses?"

I am astounded at this priest's reaction. He is so angry, at first he seems to be lost for words, and then he says "Young lady, you need to confront your father and inform him of our conversation, but you have to promise me that you will follow through with my advice. When you inform your father that you consulted with me, you also tell him that if he ever touches you again, you will contact me and I will personally make sure he suffers the consequences of his actions". He then says "You need to do this as soon as possible. If he continues to pursue you, here is my card and you must contact me immediately. I will take the necessary actions so that he will never touch you again. You must not concern yourself about being placed in an abusive foster home, since I am very familiar with many good foster homes. I will make certain that you will be taken care of properly. You are now sixteen and only have two more years to go until you can be independent; however you must promise me that you will take action immediately". He then proceeds to instruct me on how to face this situation. He says, "You must confront your father the very next time you go home. Now, you realize that I am wearing my Roman Collar, therefore I cannot divulge the information you have given me, and I can assure you that he will ask you specifically if I was wearing this vestment when you talked to me. I am not telling you to lie with your response, and will leave it to your discretion as to how you respond to this question". He added, "Also tell your father you consulted with a doctor, and he confirmed that there is absolutely nothing wrong with you, therefore if you attempt to continue with the sexual abuses, I will inform Father Flynn who will in turn report you to the proper authorities".

CHAPTER 20

CONFRONTATION WITH ABUSER

I am so angry that I feel the need to confront the old man as soon as possible. I am not due to go home for another two weeks, however since the advice from Father Flynn is so fresh in my mind and I am so angry and fully prepared for a confrontation with the old man. I return home the following weekend. When my father and I are alone and knowing from the way he is looking at me that he anticipates having his way with me again, I say, "I have something important to tell you, so please sit down and hear me out".

He replies, "Why don't we wait to talk. Let me give you your treatment first, and then we can relax and have our talk".

I say, "No, I need to talk to you right this moment, this cannot wait. It is very important you listen to me very closely".

He sits back down, and says, "OK, let's hear it."

I take a deep breath, then take out the doctor's note; hand it to him and say, "Please read the page I have just handed you".

He reads, than says, "What is this?"

I respond, "Please read, you will notice that the date stamped on this document was last week.

This was obtained from my doctor who performed a full examination and found absolutely nothing wrong with me. I am appalled and so angry to have found out that you have lied to me all these years. I am also informing you that I had a private consultation with Father Flynn, the new priest at Notre Dame. I had a long discussion regarding your actions with me, specifically the sexual abuses, and yes, I repeat sexual abuses. I have a difficult time accepting the fact that you have not only lied to me; you have used me for your own sexual satisfaction all these years. From now on, there will be no more so-called treatments."

The look on his face was pure fear. He turned completely white and the very first question he asked was, *"Was the priest wearing his Roman Collar?"*

I reply, "At the time of my consultation with the priest, I was so upset that I did not notice if he was wearing the Roman collar."

After my discussion with the old man I called Norman and asked, "Are you busy at the moment, and if not, could you give me a ride to the bus depot. I need to return to my school to complete an assignment." He readily agrees to pick me up, and since he is not busy, he personally drives me directly to my school.

During the drive, he keeps glancing at me and finally asks, "Are you feeling well, you appear upset?"

I respond "I'm fine, but I just realized that I forgot to hand in an important assignment prior to Monday to be able to receive a proper grade."

He replies, "Aileen, I think that there is more to this than what you are telling me, so if you need to discuss any problems, please feel free to talk to me".

I reply, 'Norm, I am fine, I am just upset at myself for failing to complete my schoolwork and am concerned about my grade". That answer seems to satisfy him, and he drops me off when we arrive at the school.

I do not return home for at least four weeks. There are no further words said between the old man and myself about our prior conversation and he leaves me alone for at least six months. He then finds out that I am working odd jobs on the weekends that I am home, such as babysitting and doing menial housework for neighbors. I am doing this in an attempt to earn spending money to buy myself decent clothes, which includes a specific outfit that I have been admiring, while shopping with Ellen. I am starting to take an interest in socializing with school chums and their friends.

One day, during winter break from school, as I am cleaning the house for Norman, while he is grocery shopping, the old man comes in and he hands me a beautifully wrapped gift box. I am sitting in front of the fireplace eating lunch at the time. I open the box and am so elated when I see the beautiful outfit I have been admiring in the store showcase, I am so surprised, happy and think he wants to make amends. I certainly do not anticipate what comes next. Once I get over my elation and thank him, he says, "I am so happy that you like this gift, I know it will look great on you but in order to keep this outfit, you must agree to my conditions, which are, that you continue to allow me to treat you as before, since I firmly am of the opinion the doctor did not give you a proper examination, if he had, he would have discovered that you still have a problem. I want to continue your treatment so that you can lead a normal life, be able to get married and have a family in the future. Therefore as an incentive for future treatment, you can keep the suit if you allow me to treat you until you are healed properly, and also you are to tell no one of these treatments."

The mistake he makes is giving me this gift in front of the fireplace, because the next thing he sees is the box and suit thrown into the fireplace, and going up in flames. I am so angry and he is well aware of it; no further words are necessary. He leaves the house and although I am still shaking, I am proud of myself for having handled this recent development, and hope that there will be no further advances. I return to school after the weekend is over and do not come home for at least five weeks. He, in the interim, bought me a beautiful full-length fur coat with no conditions this time. So here I am, a high school student, wearing school uniforms with a very limited wardrobe and yet given this exquisite fur coat. Ironic isn't it? The fur coat remained in the closet without ever being worn.

CHAPTER 21

MEET LIFETIME MATE

When I turn seventeen, I start dating a friend of Norman, a young man named Sam, and after a few months my father starts getting very concerned about the possibility that the relationship is becoming too serious. In the meantime, Norman also introduces me to a young Irishman named Ryan, who had recently emigrated from Ireland. At our first introduction Ryan asks me out. I am still under the age of eighteen and need my father's approval for dating, I tell the Irishman I will let him know. Since father is of the opinion I am getting too serious with Sam, he readily gives his approval to date Ryan, looking very pleased that I will be breaking up with Sam.

The next time I see Ryan, I approach him and say "You asked me for a date, and then when I said I would let you know, you never came back. Were you serious and if so, my answer is, I would be happy to join you for a movie."

Our first date did involve going to a local movie, then having coffee at the local coffee shop. Ryan is so homesick that he talks and talks to me for hours about his family in Ireland. Even though I have a difficult time understanding his Irish brogue, I can sit there and listen to him for hours. The evening is by far, the most enjoyable time I have had for a long time.

Although I am still attending the boarding school, I now decide to come home most weekends, and in lieu on depending on having someone pick me up from the school, I take the bus and am always met at the bus station by Ryan. We then take off on a date, and see each other Friday and Saturday nights. He takes me to see his Irish friends, and I soon become part of that group who meets every Friday evening, as well as join the ballroom dancing club on Saturday nights. Ryan is a great ballroom dancer who competed in ballroom dancing in Ireland, therefore he loves to dance. We also hit it off from the onset, and it does not take us long to fall in love. Within the third month of dating, we know we are meant for each other, and start discussing marriage; however I am very concerned about my father.

During one of our dates I say to Ryan; "I have something serious to tell you, so let's sit down and please hear me out".

He says, "Wow, you sound serious, so let's have it".

I then respond, "You know very little about me, except for the fact that I have lived in several different homes, but this is of a different nature. I have been sexually abused by my father". He sits not saying anything for a few minutes, then he says, "What has transpired in the past is not important, we love each other, and that's all that matters at the moment. I am not going to question you as to what has transpired however, I accept you for what you are, and know in my heart that whatever abuse you received, we will put that in the past". I am so relieved when Ryan does not inquire as to the actual facts of the abuses. He says, "I appreciate your truthfulness and honesty however let's go from there and not discuss this anymore." This removes so much pressure from me, since I am so concerned about this situation and I refuse to enter into a serious relationship without being truthful about the type of family I came from and what I have been subjected to. I want to give Ryan a chance to reconsider his proposal. It is a relief to know that Ryan does not question the extent of the sexual abuse, nor does he look down on me for having allowed these abuses.

We continue dating, and Ryan also accepts the fact that some of my siblings as well as father may have problems with the concept that we are considering marriage. They may seriously object due to the facts that Ryan is not a French Canadian, nor a Catholic. I am also concerned that Ryan's family may also object to this marriage due to the difference in religion. Ryan grew up in Northern Ireland, which is predominantly Protestant and Ryan is Protestant. When we inform my family of our plan to get married, my father is so furious once he realizes the seriousness of the relationship and our impending marriage. His reasoning is as follow: My future husband is a foreigner, an Irish immigrant; he is a Protestant and he does not speak French.

For these reasons father does not consider Ryan a proper person for me to marry and absolutely restricts me from seeing him again. Unfortunately, most of my siblings agree with him. Of course, I continue dating Ryan, and the next time I come home from my school, my father informs me, "You are to discontinue dating this Irishman". "If you do not break up the relationship I will instruct the nuns at the Academy that you are no longer allowed to leave the school grounds, for the remainder of the year. As he makes his wishes known, he gets so angry that he pounds on the kitchen table with his hand with such force, that he actually breaks a bone in his right hand. I later find out that he had a similar conversation with Ryan.

I am so upset and later have a chance to discuss the matter with Norman, who always listens to me and readily gives me advice whenever I ask. He is there for me again, and patiently sits me down and listens to me, all the while comforting me. I do not inform him of the abuses I have been subjected to by the old man, since I certainly am not prepared and am too embarrassed to inform the whole family of my father's sexual abuses. Norman says, "Look Aileen, you are a level headed young lady and are very capable of making your own decision therefore if you think that marrying Ryan is the right thing to do and are sure of yourself, then go through with it, and I am in full support. I introduced you to him, and feel the two of you will have a very good life together, however it is your decision to make." My brother makes me feel I am mature and sensible enough to make this very important decision wisely.

Fortunately my eighteenth birthday is within a week, therefore the day I turn eighteen, Ryan picks me up from the boarding school. I have already explained my dilemma to Mother Superior; she understands the situation, offers to have the nuns assist me in packing, so that I will be ready for Ryan, when he arrives. Mother Superior has known me for the last four years, and informs me that she has total confidence in my judgment, and gives me her blessing when I leave. That blessing meant a lot to me. The month is October, and since I will not be able to graduate with my class, Mother Superior request that I be present for graduation, in order that I do the honor of presenting an award, so that I will be made part of the graduation ceremony. I am honored, grateful and elated to be included in the graduation ceremony.

I have previously called Joan, who lives in Toronto, and asked if I could stay with her. She readily agrees, therefore Ryan picks me up from the school, and with Mother Superior's blessing, I leave the boarding school and move in with my sister Joan, and her family. She readily accepts Ryan and assists me in settling in Toronto, giving me advice on how to go on interviews, as well as joining me in the planning of my wedding. She even allows her daughter, who is five years old at the time, to be part of our wedding party by being our flower girl.

CHAPTER 22

WEDDING

My sister Joan is very understanding and attempts to help me in every way possible. I am still not prepared to inform her or the rest of the family about our father having used me as his sex slave, so I keep silent. I am very fortunate in being able to obtain a clerical position with an insurance company within a week after moving in with my sister. This gives me the independence I so greatly need and also gives me the opportunity of planning our wedding without any interference. It is very important to some of my siblings, as well as our father that I marry a person of my own religion, as well as a French Canadian and there appears to be so much animosity towards my future husband. Although Ryan grew up in Northern Ireland, at which time the country was in turmoil over difference in religion, he is not prejudiced in any way, and readily accept my beliefs, and never attempts to discourage me in attending Mass. Actually, since he understands that I want to be married in the Catholic Church, he readily agrees to undergo Catholic lessons, and joins the Catholic religion, so that we can be married by a priest in the Catholic Church.

Even though I have very confused feelings about my dad I am not completely comfortable with these mixed feelings. I still follow my religious teachings, such as "Honor thy Parents" and feel an obligation to ask him to the wedding and march me down the aisle, if he so desires. He did attend the wedding, along with my brothers Norman, Will and Robert. Rose, Joan and Leanne are also present. Because of the religious differences, my oldest sister Ellen refuses to attend our wedding, and keeps her daughter Celine, from attending as well. I am sad by this decision, since I am of the opinion that Ellen and I have established a great relationship, and her daughter Celine is like a little sister to me. It is difficult to explain the mind set of religious affiliations during that era.

I am fortunate that one of my roommates from the boarding school's mother is a seamstress and she graciously make my wedding dress, therefore I am able to wear a beautiful white gown. The wedding party consists of Leanne and Robert who have driven in from Montreal, Norman, and friends. Joan's five year old daughter is our flower girl. Ryan cannot not understand French and Leanne and Robert cannot not speak nor understand English, however they are still able to communicate. A small reception is given to us at a friend's home and then we leave that same evening for a three day honeymoon stay in Buffalo. This is both our very first flight, the time is approximately six o'clock in the evening and it is spectacular. When we take off the sky appears to be overcast, but soon the plane is above the white puffy clouds and it is beautiful. When we fly over Niagara Falls, the lights have just been turned on over the falls, and oh, what a spectacular sight.

We are so young and inexperienced, new adventures are exciting, however Ryan and I are in such a daze, that we did not even consider making arrangements for hotel accommodations in Buffalo. When we arrive in Buffalo, we realize that we erred in not having made these reservations. It is Memorial weekend, we suddenly find ourselves standing in front of the airport not knowing where to go. A taxi cab driver sees us looking around in front of the airport so he comes over to us and the very first word he says is "Honeymooners?"

When we respond to the affirmative, he says, "Don't worry, I know exactly where you can obtain a room within a reasonable amount, and you will find it is a very nice Hotel". The accommodations are just perfect, as well as within our budget. What luck!! On our wedding night, Ryan is very understanding with my hesitation, and is very gentle in our lovemaking. We have a great three-day honeymoon in Buffalo, sightseeing, shopping, dining in fine restaurants and thoroughly enjoying ourselves.

When we return to Toronto and we move into our first small apartment. The apartment is actually two bedrooms, upstairs of a private residence in the suburbs of Toronto. During our days of courting, the wedding, honeymoon, Ryan never mentions one word nor does he inquire about my father's sexual actions. He is very patient with me and treats me with the greatest respect. We both are fortunate to have employment; Ryan is working in aircraft and I work for an insurance company. Although Ryan and I make some attempts to reunite with my family and Ryan tries so hard to get to know everyone and be accepted, there is still so much animosity from my family. We finally limit our visits to family members realizing that it will take time for acceptance, but it bothers me a lot for us not to be accepted by my own family.

CHAPTER 23

VISIT RYAN'S FAMILY IN IRELAND

Ryan had grown up in Belfast, Northern Ireland, while it was under siege during the war, as a matter of fact Ryan remembers the bombings over Belfast, and running to the shelters. The year was 1942, and the reason Germany bombed Belfast so strongly was to destroy their harbor and ship building industry. Ryan was twelve years old at the time of the bombing, and as he assisted the English and American soldiers in taking care of the German prisoners he experienced wonderful treatment and attention from the American soldiers. They were great with children, gave them food, candy and treated the young people with respect. Although Ryan had immigrated to Canada, his primary goal was to be able to move to United States and become an American citizen because of his experiences with American military personnel.

A couple of years after our wedding, we both decide that we will attempt to move to the United States, therefore we file the proper documentation with the American Embassy, follow through with the requirements, such as passing a physical, including a blood test and lung x-rays, and obtain clearance from Canadian law enforcement, and also from Northern Ireland for Ryan, to prove that we have absolutely no outstanding criminal records. After a six month waiting period, our American Visas are granted. We then proceed to obtain our passports etc., and are prepared to leave Canada.

The day we walk out of the American Embassy with all of our necessary documents and approval to move to the United States, we locate a travel agency and book our flight to Ireland to meet my husband's family. We figure what better time to go to Ireland, since we have planned on leaving our current jobs and will have time to take a long vacation, before moving to our final destination in United States. The year is 1957.

We board for our overseas flight, and the plane is only half full, therefore we are fortunate in having room to stretch and sleep since this is an overnight flight. When the attendant comes over to take order for cocktails, I feel so mature and want to emulate the movie stars, so I order a martini. When the order arrives, it feels so sophisticated to hold this fancy martini glass, I start my drink, however in lieu of taking a small sip, and I take a huge gulp and choke on the almost straight alcohol. What a shocker that was, however it teaches me that I am not so mature after all, and that I should stop considering myself a sophisticated movie star.

Ryan's family, which includes his two sisters, Daphne and Sheila with husbands, his mother as well as his brother Reginald with wife all meet us as we disembark from our flight in Belfast. What a welcome! By this time, Ryan has been away from his family over four years. Here I am, very apprehensive and thinking the reception will be lukewarm, due to the fact I am a total unknown, a foreigner and a catholic. I am pleasantly surprised since they immediately accept and treat me as part of the family. Ryan and I stay with his mother and she is so gracious. The house in which Ryan's mother lives is the same house Ryan and siblings grew up. It is a two story house with the bedrooms upstairs, and the kitchen, the sitting room and a parlor. The sitting room is the only room with the main fireplace, and appears to be the main room for all family members to congregate. The parlor is used only when special guests are visiting. Their customs slightly differ from our Canadian style of entertaining. Whenever visitors come to the house, and this is usually without previous arrangements, the guests are always served tea with pastries. It never ceased to astound me that every household we visited always had pastries readily available, and I am not talking about normal pastries, they were always served with whipped cream; well decorated, and so delicious.

Even though we have been married two years, the entire street where Ryan had grown up surprises us with a wedding party. There are approximately thirty neighbors and what a great party. They have combined their moneys and bought us a set of Waterford glassware with a whiskey decanter, and the famous Irish Belleek clock. Now I understand why my husband did not hold any prejudices; his family is so kind and does not even mention religion, even though I am fully aware that there are many political problems between Northern and Southern Ireland, which encompasses the religion differences between the two countries. I am also aware that Ryan's older brother, Thomas holds a high position with the Orange Order, which is an anti-Catholic organization, and we had been previously been advised that if the Order found out that Ryan had married a Catholic, Thomas would be demoted in his position with the Orange Order. I was led to believe that we were not welcome in his home; however Ryan was insistent that we visit Thomas and his family. We proceed to do so. We knock on their front door prepared to accept whatever type of greetings he may give us; as he opens the door; he extends his hand to Ryan, gives me a big hug and graciously invites us into their home. Both he and his wife gave us such a great welcome, and we visited for several hours. There was never a mention of religion nor did I get any negative feelings from them. His brother was a perfect gentleman. Thomas has since passed away;

we are still in close contact with our sister in law and his children.

This is the era in which many Irish rebels attempt to disrupt, by throwing bombs, and the English military has tanks patrolling the Belfast area. While sightseeing in the city I make a serious mistake. We walk by an English tank in midtown of Belfast, which is occupied with soldiers and like the usual tourist; I take a picture of the tank and soldiers. I am immediately approached by a soldier and by the way he marches towards me with his serious demeanor I realize I have made a grave mistake. I quickly start talking to the soldier, making him fully aware that I am a foreigner in his country, so that the reprimand will be held to a minimum. He demands that I give him the camera. He then removes the roll of film and hands me the camera back with a request that I avoid taking pictures of their presence in Belfast or any location while I am touring Ireland. Since I appear so surprised by this soldier's action, he realizes I do not fully understand his action, so he takes the time to explain that some people often act as tourists, taking pictures, and then send them to the opposing party, which would divulge the soldier and perhaps endanger his life at a later time.

We treat this vacation like a second honeymoon and stay five weeks. We explore all of Northern and Southern Ireland which is classified as two separate countries and I am surprised that they use different currencies. The country is beautiful, so green, and lush. My favorite location in Belfast is Mount Stuart, which is a castle, surrounded by gardens that are spectacular consisting of several acres, with a small lake amid the garden. Many of you may have heard the following saying "while in Ireland you will meet no strangers" well that is very true. Everywhere we go everyone speaks to one another. The entire family joins us traveling to Dublin. The distance from Belfast to Dublin is approximately one hundred miles. We have a caravan of four vehicles holding the entire Irish family. As we travel to Dublin, it seems that we stop at every little town on the way. Of course every time we stop, we visit a pub and have a pint and a chat with the locals. Would you believe it has taken us a full ten hours to reach Dublin? We then visit a castle which has been renovated into an exclusive hotel in Dublin and we have the opportunity of watching their evening entertainment which includes Irish tenors, as well as young Irish dancers who are spectacular. This is a vacation not to be forgotten. We travel through the countryside enjoying the scenery, castles, and Irish cottages and of course the famous pubs.

CHAPTER 24

EMIGRATE TO CALIFORNIA

Upon our return to Canada from our "second honeymoon" trip, we prepare to finally take off for United States. We answer an ad in the paper, which requests drivers for the purpose of transporting new vehicles to different parts of the States. The year is 1957 and we are given a brand new 1957 Chevrolet to drive from Detroit to Phoenix; therefore we travel through United States in style. We are given two weeks to reach our destination so we have the luxury to stop whenever we want to see specific attractions throughout our travel across the country.

We had originally planned on settling in Santa Monica, however while working for the insurance company in Canada, I notify them of our impending move to California. Coincidentally they inform me that they have an office in San Diego; luckily they have an opening, therefore I am assured of immediate employment. Although San Diego has not been our first choice, it is pure luck that makes us settle in this beautiful city. Ryan is also aware that the aircraft factories in San Diego are seeking employees; therefore we are certain of employment for him as well. We are so fortunate to reach Phoenix safely. We then take a bus to San Diego. We have not obtained adequate information on San Diego and are completely taken by surprise upon our arrival downtown San Diego. As we disembark from the bus, we are taken aback by the amount of servicemen in the area, however all young servicemen we come across are so congenial. We had no idea that San Diego had a major military base. We arrive at six o'clock in the evening, and obtain a rental car, locate a motel and celebrate our arrival with a fancy dinner.

The next day, we attempt to locate a furnished apartment, and what a chore that is. San Diego appears to be booming, and apartments are limited. We finally locate an apartment in what appears to be an unsafe area, however decide to follow through with the rent, since it was the only one we could locate. Once we place our first month's rent, I sit down and cry, Ryan thinks that I am crying because of happiness, however I am crying due to the fact, the location appears so questionable. The next day, we drive to the insurance company, to check in for my new job, and when the proper forms are complete, I hand them over to the manager. He reviews the information, looks at us and says, "You definitely do not want to live in the location of your new apartment. What made you decide to live there?"

We respond, "We are totally unfamiliar with San Diego, so could you suggest a better area?"

He says, "I highly recommend you drive up the Avenue you are on now, then onto University Boulevard, where you will find a much safer area. They have several apartments in that location, which is very close to our famous park and you should be able to find something more to your liking". We follow his instruction and luckily we do find a much more suitable apartment, therefore we settle in that area. We then drive to the aircraft factory on Harbor Drive, and Ryan is able to obtain employment to start the next day. We return our rental car, and take the bus back to our new home. We have no vehicle, and since we are so used to the transportation in Toronto we just assume that San Diego will have a similar system. Much to our surprise, San Diego does not have a rapid transit system, therefore Ryan is forced to walk the ten miles to his new employment as well as walk the ten miles back. I am fortunate that I can take a bus to my new place of employment. Our funds have been drastically depleted due to our extended vacation; therefore we have to wait at least six to nine months in order to have enough money to buy a vehicle. We are fortunate to have the famous Balboa Park so close to our home; this gives us the opportunity to spend many weekends exploring that area, which is so beautiful.

Also, I had never been close to the ocean and find it to be so breathtaking, it seems I cannot not get enough of the waves and find it so enjoyable, therefore every week end during the summer; we take the bus and spend Saturday and Sunday sunning ourselves at the beautiful beaches. What a great first summer, and since we do not know too many people to socialize with, we spend a lot of togetherness and certainly get to know each other very well.

Within six months, we are finally settled in San Diego, but have not made any contact with my Canadian family, since most of my family did not appear to want any association with us. After approximately eight months of living in California I receive a letter which has been directed to the main office of the insurance company I work for and they kindly forwarded this letter to me. My sister Joan is making an attempt to locate us and when I receive the letter I cry. I am so happy to know at least one of my sisters cares enough to attempt to make contact. I respond and we again reunite with both Joan and Rose through letters.

We are then informed that Will is attempting a family reunion, and he contacts us and advise us of the reunion with a request we attend, as well as stay at his home during our visit. We are so pleased that we are finally being accepted and included in my family gathering, that we readily accept the invitation. It turns out to be a large gathering, between the siblings with spouses; the only one missing is Leanne and her family. Robert has since passed away at the age of 36 from cancer.

Ryan and I look forward with great anticipation to this gathering. Disappointingly, Ryan still has not been accepted by my family. The old man still has a lot of authority over the family, and they go along with recommendation in not acknowledging Ryan as part of the family and it appears as if they are going out of their way to speak only French and totally snub him. We do not really enjoy ourselves at this reunion, and realize that except for Rose, Joan and Norman, we will be limiting our association with my side of the family.

Once we return to San Diego, we decide this city will be our permanent home. One evening, Ryan arrives home from work and says, "I was talking to a coworker, and he advises me that there is a new project of small homes being built and will be readily available within the next six months, so let's take a drive and inspect the models". I am so excited, since there is a possibility of purchasing our first house. As soon as we see the models, we immediately place our down payment, and await completion of the project. Within three months, the homes are available and we move into our first house. What an exciting time that is. We then shop for furniture within our budget, so we are set to finally say, we have found our little heaven. We are very fortunate to meet our neighbors, who are also new owners, and find that they are all very amicable. A year later we have our first child, Shawn is born in June 1960, and I become a stay at home mom. By that time we are well established in the neighborhood, and have become very friendly with our neighbors, specifically Margie who lives next door with a family of five teenagers. I am very fortunate to have such a great neighbor. She takes me under her wing and assist me as well educate me in taking care of a newborn baby. She is my guardian angel and I would have been lost without her guidance. She is a true friend and it seems as if she has adopted me as an additional daughter. Not only are we fortunate in having Margie, her teens are always readily available whenever assistance is needed, such as babysitting or housework help. Our second son Patrick is born in March, 1962. During that same year, the economy appears to be at a standstill and Ryan loses his job. Although I have planned on remaining a stay at home Mom, due to our financial limitations, I return to work in the insurance industry.

CHAPTER 25

PSYCHOLOGICAL PROBLEMS

I really am proud of the fact that I have been able to handle all of my feelings regarding my childhood abuse and feel I am able to lead a normal life. However I do not fully realize that I am developing a major problem with alcohol dependency. As far as I am concerned, alcohol is part of our entertainment and a normal way of life. Therefore all appears to be going smooth in our lives. As time goes by the alcohol becomes a very important part of my life, because it has a way numbing my mind and making me forget all of the animosity, anger and hatred that have built up because of the childhood physical, mental and sexual abuses over so many years, while I am in an alcoholic stupor. My drinking becomes a nightly ritual. I fool myself into thinking that if I limit my drinking by not starting until six o'clock every evening, then I do not have a problem. Of course once I have that first drink, I usually drink until I black out. Since I always have trouble sleeping, I use the excuse that I need a drink to help me relax and sleep, but that is merely an excuse, since the alcohol is certainly not helping with the insomnia.

I am still very fortunate that I am able to function, hold down a responsible job and develop a great career in the business world. I become aware that the company I work for during the women's movement is considering training and promoting women into higher position. I take advantage of this situation and request consideration to enter the advancement program. Fortunately I am included in this program and very quickly I am able to step up to a higher position which had previously been dominated by males only.

It finally has come to a point where I cannot control my alcohol addiction and I finally realize that I have a serious problem with alcohol consumption. My husband is standing by me during my alcohol addiction, however he attempts on numerous occasions to get me to curtail the drinking. Although Ryan does not have medical nor psychological knowledge, a person does not require a degree in that field to know that a serious problem is evolving with my drinking. He finally convinces me that I need to seek assistance, therefore I check into the Alcoholic Anonymous program and what a surprise it is for me to find out how this program works. I am also astounded on the type of individuals attending these meetings. I meet some wonderful people, and find out that these meetings certainly serve their purposes.

I also meet a wonderful gal, who becomes my sponsor and after talking to me for several sessions, she convinces me to seek psychological treatments, so that I can be taught on how to release all those pent up feelings. Although I have already attempted to obtain therapy treatments, and have attended a few sessions with three separate therapists, over a period of three months, I have stopped due to complete dissatisfaction with their style of therapy. It seems that although they listen I did not obtain any satisfaction, and all they can say after I describe certain events "And how did that make you feel?" I sense total boredom on their part; therefore I cease to attempt treatments.

Once I become convinced by my sponsor that I desperately need professional help; I go on her recommendations and obtain counseling through her recommended psychologist.

My first meeting with Mona, the new therapist, is as if I have known her all my life. She insists that I call her by her first name, and I feel so comfortable talking to her. I can easily relate and divulge my childhood and teen history without embarrassment. She listens, gives advices, and she is teaching me so many things about repression of feelings, guilt, hatred, etc., and she leads me through until I can understand the reasons for my animosity, and deep rooted lack of confidence etc. At one time, as I describe the incest, I say, "Maybe it's natural for a father to love a daughter in that way".

She immediately responds. "Have you ever had that same feeling for your sons?"

I reply, "Of course not."

And she says, "Then, why do you feel it may be OK for fathers to treat their daughters in the same fashion your father treated you?" I finally realize that I should feel no guilt for hating him so much, and I need to convince myself that I did not instigate his actions. That conversation helped me considerably.

She also offers to have me hypnotized, to see if I can recall details of the sexual acts performed by the old man, hoping that this will assist me in accepting the facts that I had absolutely no control over his behavior or what I allowed him to do to my body. I refuse to be hypnotized, since I am so scared to know what he did and know the actual sexual acts he performed. I personally do not feel this information will assist me in my recovery of alcohol abuse. Through the assistance of treatments, attending meetings, friends' assistance, my sons' belief in me and my husband, who is standing by me throughout my recovery, I am able to finally stop the drinking. It takes me a while to fully understand that alcohol abuse is an illness, which can be exacerbated by physical, emotional and sexual abuses.

During my recovery, I find it very difficult in accepting the fact that I am unable to control the drinking. I have been informed that I will not be able to have even one drink of alcohol once I have stopped my drinking. One drink, I am told, will topple me over the edge and I will not be able to stop at that one drink but will continue on the binge until I pass out. Therefore I decide to test this theory. My test involves having one martini, convinced that I will be strong enough to stop after that one drink. The next thing I know, I wake up the next morning with the worst hangover I ever had; I learnt my lesson and finally fully realize the strong control of alcohol.

CHAPTER 26

FORGIVENESS

In the 1980's Ryan and I vacation to Montreal to spend some time with Leanne and her family. Her foster mother also known as "Ma Tante", my second foster mother, is now living with my sister. I have so much love for this lady. Ma Tante and I are having tea and she says to me, "Aileen, you may wish to visit your first foster mother, Maman. Papa is deceased and Maman lives in a retirement home. She wrote me recently and her letter leads me to believe she is very lonely so I am giving you her address and I highly recommend you pay her a visit; this may also assist you.

Ryan and I discuss the matter, and he agrees with Ma Tante, it would be good therapy for me to visit my foster mother and let her know I hold no animosity towards her. We decide to take Ma Tante's advice and travel to the town where Maman is living. I decided the best way to approach Maman is to call her first. When I telephone her and announce myself over the phone, I sense a great pause, then her very first comment in our telephone conversation is, "I don't want to argue with you."

I then inform her, "I am vacationing and traveling with my husband; we are in the area where you live and would like to visit with you". At first she refuses, so I respond, "I understand your feelings, and wish you well".

Then as I start to hang us I hear her say, "OK, you can visit me".

We arrive at the retirement center and knock on her apartment door. She opens her door, invites us in and at first, it is slightly awkward, and as we sit down she says, "I am so sorry that I mistreated you so badly, I did not realize this until you left. I have had many years to think about it, and cannot believe that I could have been so harsh with you. I wanted a little girl so badly, and anticipated you to be a perfect little doll. I never realized that I had a sweet child on my hands that seemed so lost and very sad, and in lieu of helping you get over the loss of your mother, I expected perfection from you. I just hope you can find it in your heart to forgive me."

I reply, "I am not here to give you a bad time, but to merely let you know that I am doing well, have a family of my own now, live in California and am leading a very happy life. When I look back of my time living with you, I realize I was not the easiest child to deal with, I showed lot of resentment about being taken away from my family, and although I agree you may have been too harsh on me, you also taught me a lot of things that I still practice to this day". We then proceed to talk about her family as well as mine, and have a wonderful visit, in which we both feel at ease and realize we have to put the past behind us and make the best of our remaining lives. We have a pleasant visit and she walks us out. As we leave and are walking away I hear her say to another senior, "She came all the way from California just to see me". It made me realize just how lonely she is. I am so glad that I had the opportunity to visit her and finally put that part of my life behind me. We finally say our goodbye with absolutely no animosity.

This visit has done a lot for me. It allows me to finally cope with that part of my life, as well as know that I have made a senior lady aware that I hold no animosity and that she has been forgiven, which also made me feel good about myself. I also feel so sorry for her, she has two sons and grandchildren, but she is living alone in a very small apartment consisting of only one room that is a combination of kitchen, bedroom and living room.

We were invited at another family reunion by Norman's son, and decided to attend, hoping that after all these years; we could reunite with my family. At one of our group family dinner, we have an open discussion involving many topics such as prior animosity etc. I make the mistake of informing Will and Norman about the sexual abuses I was put through by the old man. Will becomes so furious at me for allegedly spreading lies about his father. He vehemently refuses to believe such stories. From that time on there has been absolutely no contact from Will. Unfortunately, Norman had a heart attack in 2005, and I was informed by his son Ronald that as he laid in his hospital bed, a few days before he passed away, he told his son how bad he felt for not having protected his little sister many years ago. That made me so sad, since he possibly felt guilty for his own father's actions.

We celebrate our 50th wedding anniversary in Branson, Missouri, five years ago, along with our two sons and their families. We spend an entire week with our sons, who obtained a large condo in which we could all be together. We attended stage shows, played golf and really enjoy quality family time. We are so fortunate to have two sons, who have met wonderful gals, are married and leading productive lives. Unfortunately both sons live far from us; however we keep in touch regularly and visit whenever possible.

CHAPTER 27

RETIREMENT

Ryan and I are both retired, and enjoying being able to travel, take care of our two little Yorkies, and enjoy our remaining life in a great environment. We just returned from a vacation in Alaska visiting our oldest son and his family. It was wonderful spending quality time with the grandchildren, and be driven around that great State. We are now anticipating a visit from our other son, along with his family, and we will again enjoy family time.

I feel so grateful that I survived the childhood era, and have been able to enjoy life to the fullest. I am also very thankful and feel so fortunate that my husband stood by my side our entire life together, and specifically the time of my alcoholism; gave me full support during recovery and never gave up on me. If he as well as our sons had not been so supportive, I seriously doubt if I could have accomplished the recovery. The acceptance of my alcohol problem by our sons was also a major factor in my recovery, because they appeared to have so much confidence that I would recover from this illness, that it gave me additional incentive to make them proud of me.

Ryan was the major factor in my recovery. His confidence and belief in me gave me just the right incentive to work this through. He stood by me, took care of me at my lowest time, refused to allow me to feel sorry for myself during my recovery, seldom left me on my own, specifically when he noticed that I was getting depressed. I seriously doubt I could have made it through without his love and understanding. I am also fortunate that I was able to obtain proper counseling, to finally put the past "on its own proper shelf of past memories".

A few years ago, I had a business lunch with two ladies, who had accomplished very good positions in their business life and during this luncheon; all they could talk about was their overbearing mothers. I would have liked to have told them what life would have been like without their mothers. So many young people fail to realize the importance of having loving parents in their lives. Most people do not fully realize the impact of having a normal family life growing up, until they have families of their own.

I also hope this story will help open avenues to anyone who has had a problematic childhood and is having difficulties dealing with past. It is so important to realize horrific events can be overcome through perseverance, willingness to seek and accept assistance; attempt to come to term with their past, and become aware that there can be a hopeful future.

Sometimes we just need to read about "someone like me" to begin to seek out the needed help to heal.